Mama Dip's Kitchen

Mama Dip's Kitchen

Mildred Council

The
University
of North
Carolina
Press

Chapel Hill
and London

© 1999 The University of North Carolina Press

All rights reserved

Designed by April Leidig-Higgins

Set in Monotype Bulmer by Eric M. Brooks

Manufactured in the United States of America

This book was published with the assistance of the Blythe Family Fund of the University of North Carolina Press.

The paper in this book meets the guidelines for permanence and durability of the Committee on Production Guidelines for Book Longevity of the Council on Library Resources.

Library of Congress Cataloging-in-Publication Data
Council, Mildred. Mama Dip's Kitchen / by Mildred Council.   p. cm.   Includes index.
ISBN 0-8078-2508-5 (cloth: alk. paper)
ISBN 0-8078-4790-9 (pbk.: alk. paper)
1. Cookery, American.   2. Mama Dip's Kitchen (Restaurant)   I. Title.
TX715.C8583 1999 641.5973—dc21 99-19973 CIP

Original illustrations by Claudia McGehee.
Photographs courtesy of Tom Finn.
cloth   06 05 04 03 02   9 8 7 6 5
paper   06 05 04 03 02   15 14 13 12 11

This book is dedicated to my children, for eating what was put on the table, even if it wasn't what they liked. To the girls—Norma, Julia, Sandra, Annette, and Anita—for housekeeping while I worked; to the boys—Geary, Joe, and William—for caddying at the golf course to help put food on the table; to Roy (deceased) for being the house dad; and to my 20 grandchildren and 16 great-grandchildren with love. May God bless you all.

Contents

Acknowledgments

I want to thank God for my children, not only my birth children but also the children who would wander into my yard and to my table for a bite of food, no matter how little there was. Thanks to Roland Giduz for his encouragement and for typing all those papers after I misplaced the computer disk containing the recipes for this book. I've spent many hours in his home over the years, cooking and tending children and, in recent years, making my country chicken for his grown-up family. Thanks to Judie Birchfield for her understanding and commitment and for the time she gave in so many ways to this book. Thanks to her children, Shawn and Chelsea, for playing so nicely while we flipped so many pages. Thank you also to Tom Finn for taking the time to photograph me and the area where I grew up. I also want to express my appreciation to Susan McDonald for the support and encouragement she gave and to Jeaneane Williams for all the typing and work that she did. Thank you also to all my customers at Mama Dip's Kitchen who said that I needed to write down my recipes and never gave up hope that it could be done, even if I had to work seven days a week. And finally, thanks to Craig Claiborne for saying in 1987, "You should write a cookbook!" "A cookbook?" I said.

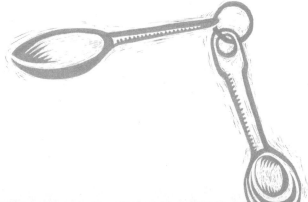

Grace

Sometimes I think that my life is a lot like a pumpkin seed. Many years ago I took a pumpkin seed—one of God's ugliest seeds—and planted it in the earth. In a few days it sprouted two green leaves. I chopped, tilled, watered, and fed it. The rain fell on it, and I tilled it again, and soon I had a long vine with blooms on it growing everywhere. By Halloween time I had two pumpkins, one small and one large.

I made a snaggle-toothed jack-o'-lantern out of the big one, scooping it out through the cut-off top and placing a broken candle inside. When I called the children in to see it, they could see the light of life shining in its ugly face. I peeled and cooked the other pumpkin and made pies and bread, which I shared with neighbors and some of the sick and shut-ins. But I still had all of these seeds left, so I put them in a pan out on the back steps. As I looked out the window later, I saw a bird, a squirrel, a butterfly, and even a bumblebee come and sit on the seeds. And I said to myself, "Heavenly Father, look what your ugly seeds have done. They have made children, my neighbors, the sick, the birds, bees, squirrels, and butterflies all happy."

This made me realize something I have thought about so many times since. My life, through this pumpkin seed, brought so much happiness and joy. Like the pumpkin seed, my life can continue to bring happiness and joy to others.

When I plant my garden in the spring, I do it with the thought that one single bean can create so many new beans—half a pound or more. How many plants will come from one bean if you chop it, feed it, and water it?

One spring, as I walked across my yard, I noticed a flower growing that I didn't even plant. One of the birds had probably dropped the seed from which it grew. I felt sorry that the bird had lost some food that may have been meant for its babies. So I dug up the plant and replanted it in my garden, while I gave silent thanks both to God and to the bird.

We don't eat flowers, but I plant them in my garden with the thought of life and beauty, which is what they represent. They represent love, happiness, and concern. When you see a bundle of flowers, your eyes light up, even if they are not for you. Flowers are like thoughts and people because there are so many kinds and colors and different names for them.

When I went to cash the first paycheck I ever got for cooking, the grocery store cashier pushed it back over the counter to me and said I would have to sign my name on the back of it. I realized then that my name was my earthly soul, which needed to be tended like the pumpkin seed—tended, tilled, fed, and harvested, to have a good life. And that's what I've tried to do ever since for my family and myself.

Mama Dip's Kitchen

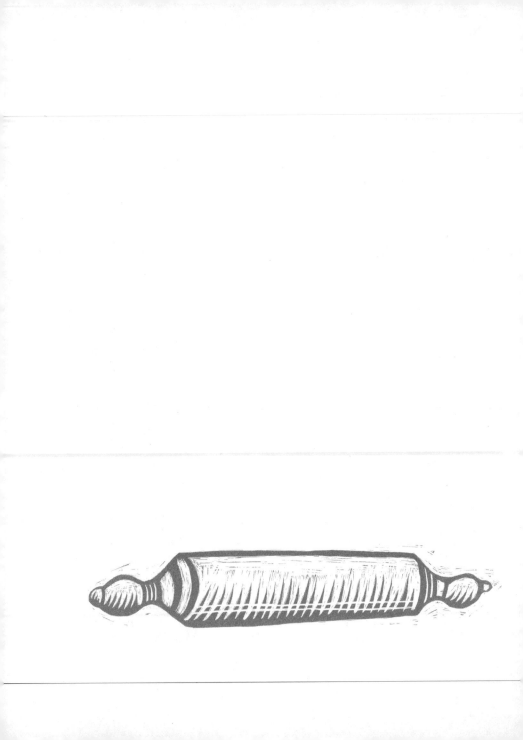

Introduction

A Life of Cooking,
1938—1999

I was born a colored baby girl in Chatham County, North Carolina, to Ed Cotton and Effie Edwards Cotton; grew up a Negro in my youth; lived my adult life black; and am now a 70-year-old American. I have always known myself as Mildred Edna Cotton Council. The cultural names haven't changed my feelings of being an American citizen. I have experienced the Negro or black American cultural world in a tiny area of the United States of America. I grew up and lived in poverty most of my life without knowing it. My children, too, grew up in poverty never knowing that they were poor. Our house just leaked. No screen doors. An outdoor bathroom and little money.

Our family was happy to sit around the table at dinner time, eating, poking jokes, and having fun. It didn't matter if the dishes and the cups didn't match. (Sometimes just a pie pan would do.) Early childhood experience equipped me to raise my children to accept life by being happy, learning about life and its struggles and disappointments.

I was raised on a farm in Baldwin Township, Chatham County, where I started cooking at an early age. Before that, I could only pretend to cook and feed the dolls that I made out of bottles and wood moss with corn silk for their long hair. I would sing and shout to my dolls and feed them mud pies. Many years later, I changed the mud pie recipe to edible ingredients and created a new dessert for my restaurant. The coconut and nuts always remind me of the small rocks and sticks that would be in the dirt mixed with water that I served to my corn silk dolls. My dolls could never tell me how well I was doing for them, but I felt they were happy because the following year, when the corn came up and made silk, the bottle dolls would be where I had left them.

Then one morning in about 1938, when I would have been around nine, Papa said the words that made me so happy. As our whole family started out to the field that morning after breakfast for the plowing and planting, he looked at me and said, "You stay here and fix a little something to eat."

I was the youngest of seven children. My mother died at the early age of 34, when I was only 23 months old and my oldest sister Bernice was just 11. Papa didn't talk about Mama to us. The few words he said were that she went to God in heaven and that she wanted him to keep all of her children together, the boys too.

Until I started doing the cooking, it had been done by one of my older sisters or by Roland Norwood, a family friend who came to live with us and helped with the washing and chores. We lived in a two-story house with a long porch and a fireplace in the kitchen and a sitting room. The porch had a swing hung from the ceiling, and when we'd swing on it, it made a noise like a crane croaking. The sitting room had a big bed, standing tall with fresh wheat straw that was stuffed into a homemade cover, making a mattress that we called a bed tick. The cover was made from unbleached flour or chicken sacks sewed together with thread that had been carefully taken out of the top of the sacks and wound around a homemade spool to keep it from tangling. The upstairs was more like a loft. You could stand up only in the middle of it. The beds were placed so their heads were under the lowest part of the ceiling. Trunks where we stored the quilts stood in every corner. The dining room had a built-in pantry with a window front and two doors whose knobs for closing the pantry at the bottom had been homemade from thread spools carved into button shapes. The top shelves were filled with pretty glasses and plates and bowls.

Mildred "Mama Dip" Council.

We had a well in the yard that would sometimes go dry in the summer. Then we would use water out of the spring down the hill, or Papa would set big tin oil drums, some holding 100 gallons, and potbellied wine barrels on rocks at each corner of the house to catch all the rain possible for washing our clothes. When the water was low in the barrels, I learned how to take the gourd dipper, jump up, hang over with my belly button on the rim of the barrel, and dip out the water.

I was called "Dip" by my brothers and sisters from an early age because I was so tall (today, I'm six feet, one inch) and had such long arms that I could reach way down in the rain barrel to scoop up a big dipperful of water when the level was low. Filling up water buckets for the kitchen had its benefits, though, as it was on my trips in and out of the kitchen with water that I first learned to cook, watching how Roland or my older sisters made things with their "dump cooking" methods and making mental notes about how ingredients went together.

Dump cooking means no recipes, just measure by eye and feel and taste and testing. Cooking by feel and taste has been a heritage among black American women since slavery, and that's the way I learned to cook. When I talk about dump cooking I am thinking of fresh vegetables (planting and tending a vegetable patch and then cooking and canning its products has also been a tradition for black women), homegrown or from a farmers' market. I think of peeling potatoes, stringing beans, chopping onions, hulling peas, washing greens, and more. Farm fresh is the highlight of country dump cooking. If you buy food too far ahead, it's not fresh when you cook it. Some vegetables keep a long time when refrigerated, but remember, usually they have already been refrigerated before you buy them.

Fruit for cobblers or pies was picked by all the children. We would just taste the fruit for sweetness and add the amount of sugar that we felt was needed. For more sweet fruit and for country pie taste, a little salt was always added to mellow the sugar with the fruit.

Vegetables were a pan or basket full or a head or two of cabbage, ears of corn, a small bucket of potatoes, with a piece of meat for each person. Measuring cups were not found in our kitchen. I learned to pinch the salt or pour it in the palm of my hand. Then I would taste the juice from the pot like Roland did. Measuring by eye or feel, I still find that my hands serve well for this, and tasting gives your pot that personal touch. After I left home, I had no measuring cups or spoons in my kitchen (salt and pepper were used right out of the container) until my children began to cook. Even then, I encouraged them not to rely on measurements too much. I would tell them to try learning to pour salt or pepper into their hands and then dumping it into the pot.

When Papa said the wonderful words to me at age nine that I could have my "turn in the kitchen," I had already been dreaming about cooking, and I could hardly wait to tell my playmates across the meadow branch that I wouldn't have time to play hopscotch or jump rope any-

Mama Dip inspecting produce at the farmers' market in Carrboro, North Carolina.

more because I had to fix dinner. I felt grown. I wanted to tell someone right then, but I knew it would take me an hour to go across the meadow branch, so I just went to the woodpile and got chips and bark to start my fire in the wood cookstove.

The fire was hard to start, and I blew and blew on it until I was dizzy. I wanted to fix a big, good meal, but all we had was whippoorwill peas and ham bone. I took the ham bone out to the woodpile to cut it into pieces with an ax, just like Roland or Papa would do. That's when I heard the guinea hens cackling down behind the house. I was sure I'd be able to get some eggs. I was so excited I even took them out of the nest with my hands, against Papa's rules. He said the guineas would never lay

Mama Dip measuring out flour with her hands, as she learned to do in dump cooking.

in the nest again if you did that. I didn't care. I just wanted to make an egg custard pie with a crust rolled out with a glass and flavored with the scrapings from the whole nutmeg that the Watkins man sold on his travels from farm to farm. That day even my cornbread turned out good – not too much soda, just like Papa had said.

In looking back now, I guess life was not easy for our family. I didn't even realize I'd grown up in a single-parent household for many years. And I know Papa sometimes had a hard time making ends meet. One year right after the Depression, Papa could barely put food on the table after the boll weevils ate up most of his cotton crop. But he always started out each morning at breakfast with the blessing, "Thank you, Father, for the food that we are about to receive for the nourishment of our bodies. For Christ's sake. Amen."

Our day began as soon as the roosters crowed, about 5:00 A.M. We never needed an alarm clock. At an early age I could tell which rooster was crowing (the guineas would make the most noise in the winter). Papa would call us by name until we stirred. A fire had to be made, breakfast started, and the cows fed and milked while it was still dark. The lantern always hung at the back door for the early morning feedings. The white wash pan with a red rim sat on a little homemade table that Papa made with slabs from the sawmill and then covered with tin. The towel hung on a nail at the back door by the wash pan. It had been bleached almost white and then hemmed, but you could still read the name of what was sold in the sack. Roland or Papa would pour hot water from the kettle and dip cold water from the bucket to make it warm. We all washed our faces and hands in the same water, patting water all over our faces, and then we all dried ourselves with the same towel, picking out a dry spot, which was hard to do if you were the sixth or seventh to use the towel. Then it was breakfast and time to get ready for school or work.

The barn was across the road from the house. A big barn, it had two sections with a covered opening in the middle where the wagon sat and where the mules could be hitched and unhitched. In the winter, Papa would wrap our legs in burlap feed sacks and tie them on with brown twine like a small fuzzy rope that was bought for bundling the wheat, oats, and fodder. Fodder is the leaves and tops of corn plants that were fed to the cows and mules in the winter months when there was no grass or honeysuckle. When you got to the barn, stray cats would come around mousing and the dogs would come looking for a treat. You had to give them a little treat. I would take the cow's tit and squeeze milk into the cat's or dog's mouth. They would catch this good, warm milk. The cats would wipe their mouths with their paws and lick them clean. The dogs would sit and lift their ears and hold their heads to the side looking for more.

It was fun how they could really catch the string of milk. But Papa knew how much milk the cow would give, so you couldn't have too much fun. He would ask, "Did you drain that cow's tits?" (The cream seems to be at the end of the milking.) The answer would be "Yessir, Papa," and then Papa would say, "Now y'all know you gonna want to make snow cream and milk shakes."

Saturdays were always the day for cleaning house with homemade equipment, like a mop made of burlap sacks tied around a hoe, or washing and boiling clothes in a big black pot with homemade lye soap. Weekdays were the time for outdoor work on a big farm in Chatham County or for heading for school, all depending on what time of year it was. In the early spring, our work might be planting Irish potatoes. We would bring the potatoes saved from the year before out from under a pile of sawdust, tow sacks, and scrap tin, sprouting them in the light before cutting out the "eyes" and then planting them in a corner of the garden.

The walnut and hickory trees were part of the shade trees in the backyard. We would gather the smaller nuts from these trees and store them in the smokehouse. In the winter we would crack them and pick out the meat with a safety pin or small nail. When we sat by the fire or when the weather was bad, we would eat the nuts, and it was like eating hard candy.

In late summer—the dog days, we called them—our work might be thinning the long vines off the sweet potatoes. We thinned out the vines because Papa said "we would only have little, stringy potatoes" if we didn't. We fed the vines to the hogs. Spring and summer were canning and preserving time for the fruits and vegetables we grew, as well as for wild things like strawberries, dewberries, blackberries, gooseberries, and muscadine grapes.

Strawberries were the first fruit to come along in the spring. My Aunt Laura and Uncle Jim were the only people I knew who had a cultivated strawberry patch. We always just found them in the pine thickets and straw fields that were untended or unplowed. We would pinch off the whole stem and take them home and make jam or strawberry butter rolls (they would be called crepes now).

The dewberry was also an early berry that we picked in some areas every year. Papa said that the dew where they grew made them sweeter, and they were sweeter still since they were always picked in the morning. We got only one or two dewberry pies or cobblers every year.

Blackberries grew most everywhere, but the biggest and best were down in the meadow edge of the pasture where it stayed damp all the time, where the cows stood and chewed their cud under the trees. We picked pecks and pecks of berries, canning cases of them for winter pies and making jam and that famous blackberry wine that we all got a little sip of on Christmas morning at the breakfast table.

Asparagus also came in the early spring. The asparagus was reserved for the men who were the head of the household, as there were only a few of those funny looking sticks that grew together. Aunt Laura would mix them with garden peas and put in milk and butter and thicken them with flour paste. We could never have any. When we visited Aunt Laura and that dish was on the table, it would smell so good. I would pretend that I had a stomachache until everyone had finished eating so I could get the leftovers in that bowl.

In the fall, we would comb the woods for muscadine grapes, which grew wild on vines up in the trees. They too were preserved for the winter. We always cut off some of the vines to make jump ropes. Fall was also the time when there were field peas. No one was ever too young to pick cotton or dried peas. We put them in burlap sacks, then emptied them onto sheets and beat them with a wooden mallet until they were to be hulled. One of us would hold the peas up high and let them fall to another sheet, while the other one fanned them to blow out the small pieces of hull. The faster you fanned, the cleaner they got.

In August and September, apples had to be canned or else sliced and dried in the sun for making pies in the winter. Later, the corn had to be shelled and cut off the cob and measured in bushels to be ground at the mill for cornmeal. We grew a type of corn that we called Trucker's Flavor (though some people called it Trucker's Favorite), and if the season was right, we could have fresh corn on the cob by the Fourth of July. Corn-bread was on the table at each meal, but it was cooked in different ways: dog bread, milk bread, pone bread, fried bread, molasses bread, and clabber bread, which has a sour taste. The dog bread was put on the table each morning six days a week, cooked in a round cast-iron pan and cut like a pie to serve each person at the table. It was the bread of family ties. It was made with meal and water, and the pan was sprinkled with corn-meal to brown the bread and keep it from sticking. Each person had a choice of molasses, honey, jelly, milk, or brown gravy to help carry it down before the biscuits. Our hound dogs, Leed and Raddler, would sometimes help out eating some of the dog bread when they wandered into the kitchen at breakfast time. You had to feed them carefully, though, or you would be told on by your brothers or sisters or threatened with having to do their every command.

In the winter, it was hog killing time. This was an occasion all by itself, but it was also the way we put food on the table for all three meals all through the year. Nothing was wasted. The hams went to the landlord, but the streaky meat and the bacon were cured and hung in the smoke-house. There was also tenderloin, back bones and spare ribs, chitlins, sausage, and souse meat (pickled parts of the pig).

We used the whole hog. Lard was made from the fat of the pigs. The fat would be cut into small pieces and cooked in a big black pot outside until it was brown and crispy and then strained with a homemade strainer made of screen wire on a pole. After they cooled, those pieces we called "cracklings" could be added to cornmeal. Even the hog's head was cut and salted down to be cured and cut into small pieces with the ax at the wood pile. The hog jowl was kept until New Year's Day for the special meal always prepared that day—hog jowl, greens, black-eyed peas, baked sweet potatoes, and crackling cornbread. The hog jowl was eaten to ward off evil spirits; the greens represented dollar bills for the New Year; and the black-eyed peas represented silver coins.

Always the cows had to be fed and milked and the milk churned. Churning the milk to make butter had to be done twice a week and sometimes three in the spring. When the grass grew faster, there were more honeysuckles there for the cows, and therefore we had more milk. We poured the milk through a strainer into a stone three-gallon jar that was covered and left alone for two or three days. The milk would be curdled. We called it clabber. The yellow part would come to the top, and then it would be ready to be churned to make butter.

Our first churn was a wood box that sat on an X-shaped cradle that hung on flat pieces of iron that swung back and forth with a handle on both ends so that two people could either push or pull on the top. It had a square hole, cut with a lid, where you poured the milk in. After pushing and pulling for 30 minutes or more you could open up the lid and see butter forming on the top. You would take off the butter in a bowl, paddle all of the milk out, and drain the churn. The milk would be called buttermilk. Then we would "work" or knead the liquid out of the butter, put it into a wooden mold, and, when it cooled, press it to make a pound of butter with a star on top.

In the summer, when the butter had cooled and we pressed it into the mold, we had to take the pats outside and put them down the well, wrapped in flour sacks to keep them cool and fresh, since we didn't have an icebox. If we made lemonade or ice cream for special occasions, Papa hitched the mule and rode about eight miles on the wagon to buy big hunks of ice, which he'd bring home wrapped in a burlap sack under a sawdust heap. In the early 1940s margarine came to the grocery stores in pound blocks of white, lard-looking stuff with no smell. In each block was a small package of deep orange coloring that needed to be mixed into the margarine to make it look like butter.

Of course the chickens had to be fed and the eggs gathered every day from the nests built along the side of the corn crib. Nowadays, most people don't even know about different kinds of chickens, but on our farm we raised Dominickers, Rhode Island Reds, and White Leghorns. Each had its own color of eggs and its own size. The Leghorns grew faster, so we ate more of them, but the Rhode Island Reds, with their shiny maroon and black feathers, were the prettiest. The guineas were pretty and were used kind of like watchdogs on every farm, but they were also particular about their eggs and were almost never eaten. We had bantam chickens too, but just for their beauty.

The work was hard, but we were always a happy family. I don't think Papa wanted us to see the pain that people talked about later in growing up. He was our assurance, and he dedicated his life to his seven children, as well as several other children, during and after the Depression. I guess he didn't want to think about how much better life would have been if Mama had lived. She had gone to Bennett College and was a teacher at Baldwin School, a one-room school that I later attended.

Papa himself had lived in New York City in the early 1900s, working during the day and learning notes and music at night to become a voice teacher. Many nights he told us stories about how he made money hand clapping music for the "buck dancing" that was held in basements of buildings in New York. He always cherished the gold pocket watch he bought when he was there and the tuning fork he used to start a song. Papa was well known around Baldwin Township. He was a steward in the church and led the choir. If someone stuttered, Papa would train him not to do it. He had everybody in Baldwin Township singing, and some of the people he taught to sing are still singing today in their eighties.

When food was short, we had fun just seeing each other spread food all over the plate so it looked like a lot and counting how many biscuits each of us ate. If the butter gave out before it got to you, you had to sop your biscuits with side meat or put shoulder grease in your molasses and sop your biscuits in that.

Breakfast was a hearty meal on the farm. All kinds of meat were eaten — mostly rabbit, squirrel, chicken, side meat, shoulders, or fish — served with milk gravy and flour jacks (pancakes). Stewed corn was a summer breakfast dish, and we also ate rice and oatmeal.

Dinner was the 12 o'clock meal. If we were working in the fields or on another farm, we would pack a dinner—which might be side meat, yams, fried Irish potatoes with onions, and canned sausage or tenderloin stuffed in biscuits—that had been cooked while fixing breakfast and put in a basket to sit in the front of the wagon away from the dogs.

If we were working near the house, a bone or ham hock would be put on the stove to cook along with breakfast. Someone would leave the field about 11:00 to go and fix dinner—fresh vegetables or dried beans and cornbread with buttermilk. Sweet milk was drunk only on Saturday and Sunday. The dinner bell in the yard would announce that the meal was ready. It was rung at the noon meal and at no other time unless there was something wrong.

Supper was the night meal, the smallest of the day. Leftovers from dinner were always kept under the sack cover on the table to be eaten with fresh cornbread and biscuits. Middling side meat, which is meat with a streak of lean and a streak of fat, might be fried, and fresh or home-canned peaches or apples might be added, along with scrambled eggs if the hens had been laying a lot of eggs. Sweet potatoes and ash cake—made from flour, cornmeal, and milk—were often cooked in the fireplace in winter. Ash cake was especially good with blackbirds that we trapped at the corn crib and roasted on wire clothes hangers in the hot fireplace ashes.

We still had plenty of fun even after our hard work. In the summer, there was fishing in the daytime and "frog gigging" at night, where you shine a light on the frogs and grab them with your hands for eating frog legs. We fished with fishhooks we made from safety pins or barbed wire and poles we cut from willow trees near the branch. Because I couldn't swim, I could fish only in the meadow branch sitting on a flat rock. But I caught little horny heads and perch there, and when we put all our fish together, we would have a "mess" of them—enough to make a meal.

In the winter, we made molasses taffy and popped corn from our own fields, or we made milk shakes from the icicles that froze from rain running off the edge of the roof. In the corner of the house there would be long icicles. We would put them in milk with vanilla and sugar and drink the mixture with a spoon. Each spoonful would have a piece of ice, and we would let the ice roll around in our mouths and then let it fall back into the jar or glass until it was all gone.

We even made our own sleds, wagons, and scooters, as well as our own dolls, popguns, and beanshooters. To make a popgun, we would cut a piece of a bush near the creek that had a soft, pithy center. We would take the soft part out with a nail and wire and make a peg from the dogwood tree that would fit in the hole. We stuffed cedar bobs in the hole; then we stuck the peg in, and the bobs would pop out 10 to 12 feet. We also made slingshots from dogwood limbs and old car inner tubes cut into strips. Beanshooters were a lot like slingshots. We made them by cutting the tongue out of an old shoe and attaching it, by means of strips cut from an old inner tube, to a piece of dogwood limb in the shape of a Y. We played music with harps that we made with a piece of paper over a comb. One year Papa bought a Victrola, and we would play blues, sad songs, and gospel quartets.

When I was little, Papa would put me on his knee as if his knee was a horse and bump me up and down, and sometimes he would make such music with his mouth that it made me curious to pull his mouth open to see what was making that pretty sound. Like all children, we did things we never told about when we were by ourselves—smoking rabbit tobacco, a wild herb that we found in the straw field, until it made our heads swim, or sneaking eggs to school to trade for cookies and soda at the store on our way home.

When it was time to go upstairs to bed, my brothers and sisters would take turns carrying the lamp, often playing scary jokes on each other when the lamp had been blown out by the last person. The screech owl and hoot owl would sometimes let out their cries, and then we'd really fight for cover. Being the youngest and just a baby when Mama died, I slept at the bottom of Papa's bed. Every night we had to say our prayers, and I'd finish my "Now I lay me down to sleep" long before Papa, down on his knees at the foot of the bed, would finish his. Sometimes I'd scoot over to the side of the bed to see if I could hear what he was saying. At times he was praying it wouldn't start raining because the roof leaked so bad and we'd have to move our bed to keep from getting wet. When I was young I remember wanting to ask him if I could help because it took him so long to say his prayers.

Sundays were special at our house. Even the blessing Papa said was special: "I want to thank You for watching over us while we slumbered and slept." And breakfast on Sunday was flapjacks with chicken and gravy.

On the second and fourth Sundays of warm months, we'd go to Uncle Jim and Aunt Laura's after church. Uncle Jim was Papa's brother, and he and Aunt Laura lived six miles from us. They lived better than most people I knew then, because Uncle Jim lived at my grandfather's homeplace. Therefore, Uncle Jim did not have to share his crops with a landlord the way Papa and most black people did at that time. Uncle Jim and Aunt Laura never had children, but Aunt Laura loved us as her own. Aunt Laura always let everybody know that "These is Papa Buddy's children, and he's raising all them young'uns by himself, so make sure they get something to eat" whenever there was homecoming dinner at church.

Aunt Laura was a queen to all the children at church, but she was really special to us. She always made our three Christmas cakes — molasses, raisin, and butterscotch. When we were at her house, we were always happy to fill up the cookstove wood box because she'd give us a ham biscuit that had been mellowed in the redeye gravy left over from breakfast. We never had to eat out of pie pans at her house as we often did at home. Aunt Laura would let me set the table with bone-handle knives, forks, and spoons, and she even had a pretty tablecloth made from big spools of twine that was like the thread they used for quilting sometimes (this would be called crochet nowadays). We had to help her pick the seeds out of the cotton to spread in the quilts. Sometimes she would use cut-up overalls for the padding.

I always hated it when summer was over because we didn't go to Uncle Jim and Aunt Laura's much in the winter. But they would come to visit us and bring outing slips and bloomers, quilts, sheets and pillow cases, all made from feed sacks, to help Papa in providing for his seven children, since they didn't have any children of their own.

The second Sunday in August was the time for one of my favorite occasions—the homecoming feast at Hamlet Chapel Colored Methodist Episcopal Church (after the civil rights movement, its name was changed to Hamlet Chapel Methodist Episcopal Christian Church). The women dressed so gracefully with their handmade broomstick shirtwaist dresses covered by starched and ironed feed sack aprons to keep their dresses clean. Their hair would be shining with grease and rolled up with hair pins, with a straw hat pressing on their forehead. They served dinner on a long wooden table nailed between two cedar trees near the church well and laughed and chattered as they spread fried chicken and vegetables of every kind on the table, cutting up pies and cakes to feed an army of hungry men, women, and children. This was a great time in between plowing, hoeing, and picking, and I longed to be able to cook good things for people to eat from my earliest memories.

One special Sunday, when I was supposed to give a recitation in church, I had my hair straightened, and everyone wanted to touch it. My dress was pink dotted swiss, with sashes tied into a bow in the back. My new shoes were black patent leather ones that my sister had bought from Berman's store on Franklin Street in downtown Chapel Hill. When I put the shoes on that morning, I knew that they were too little, but my heart would not let me admit that they were not big enough. By the time we got

Mama Dip at Hamlet Chapel Methodist Episcopal Christian Church in Chatham County, beside a table that is covered with delicious dishes during homecoming or other church social events.

to church, when I put my feet on the ground, I had to walk on the side of my pretty shoes.

Uncle Abe Burnette—not our real uncle but a neighbor who lived across the meadow branch—made corn hominy, fireplace chairs and benches, rocking chairs, and molasses. His molasses mill was one of my favorite things. He made a big vat that was on an axle and wheel. He would hook a mule to a long wooden tongue sticking out from the vat. We would cut the cane from our patch and take it over to his mill. The mule would go round and round, mashing the juice from the cane that we had cut. The cane juice would be stirred and cooked in large flat pans, sometimes way into the night, so it wouldn't stick. Then it would be put in jugs, and Uncle Abe would take a share for grinding and making it.

The molasses would be stored in the loft over the kitchen. We kept things like the molasses—as well as some vegetables, fruits, and wine—there so they wouldn't freeze. The loft was just three or four planks left unnailed in the ceiling so you could reach in if you stood on a chair and get what you wanted. By spring, all the canned goods would be gone, but there was always plenty of molasses, and sometimes honey that had been gathered by Papa and other men from trees after they smoked the bees away in the dark of night.

To make hominy, Uncle Abe placed corn kernels in wooden tubs and covered them with hay and ashes from the fireplace. He added a little water every day for nine days. The ash water took the husks off the corn, and then the corn was washed over and over again until it was clean and white.

We had all started to school at Baldwin School, a one-room school built of planks that had never been painted. The potbellied stove, with its long pipe through the ceiling and roof, stood almost in the middle of the room, near the teacher's desk. One teacher taught all grades. We all studied, ate lunch, and got out of school at the same time. There were four windows and a front and back door. The back door was used only by the boys bringing in wood for the stove or water from the spring.

When my sister Myrtle—we always called her "Big Baby" or just "Big"—got very sick and was put in a plaster body cast after an 18-month stay at Duke Hospital, we all had to take turns going to school so somebody could stay with her. Infantile paralysis, or polio as it was later called, kept her in a cast for two years until it was removed and she could learn to walk again. Whoever went to school brought the lessons home for the others, so we all kept learning, including Big. The same thing would happen when harvest time came and family members or neighbors had to stay out of school to help with the crops. Someone would let them know what we had in school, and we would all get together and play "teacher" or make up learning games. We would rake the yard real clean and work out arithmetic problems with a dried dogwood limb or choose sides and call out spelling words. Even if you missed days in school, you didn't miss learning. On the weekend, sometimes Papa would bring back candy sticks or cheese and crackers from the store for treats because we helped one another. We all learned to read and spell, and my brothers could work any kind of math.

When Baldwin School closed, my family moved about four miles down the road to be on the bus route to Pittsboro's Horton High School. The farm was much smaller, but Papa said the soil was better, and, most important, the landlord wanted only a quarter of the harvest. Our old landlord had gotten half the harvest. Things were hard there. Papa even accepted some of Roosevelt's WPA food one time. But when it was delivered to us, they brought so much that it took up half the front porch where they stacked it, and some of it was so strange—brown flour (whole wheat, I guess now, but we'd never seen it before), canned meat, and yellow cornmeal (we'd always had white meal)—that Papa said, "Thank you but don't bring any more; it'll take me a long time to use all this."

On the new farm we grew watermelons, cantaloupes, peas, and lima beans, which we sold to the Creel Store on Franklin Street in Chapel Hill. I started washing and ironing for the new landlord, though I was still cooking and canning for the family, as well as helping with the plowing and the planting. I loved to plow the field until the planes started zooming so low overhead after World War II started. Times were really hard then. My oldest sister Bernice, who had a job in Chapel Hill, helped us some, but she wanted to get married and would need her money for herself.

We worked the new farm for two years, but after Papa sold the timber on his family's homeplace, we moved back to Papa's home farm near Uncle Jim and built a new log cabin to live in. World War II took two of my older brothers into the service. By then, tobacco had become the crop to grow. But the first year we planted tobacco the government came and cut down two long rows because Papa had gone over his allotment.

Soon after that harvest, in 1945, Papa bought a house in Chapel Hill. Big Myrtle and her son, Roy, lived with us for some years, and Roy had become sick and needed care. We didn't have a car, so we moved to town where he could get the help he needed. When Big died in 1948, Roy became like my own child, and he lived wherever I lived until his death.

When Papa made up his mind that we would move to Chapel Hill, I was really upset. When I had been to town with him before, I'd seen girls in bobby socks, pleated skirts, and sweaters, with shiny combs and magnolias in their hair, and I just couldn't see myself sitting in a classroom with them. My grandmother Martha, a midwife in Durham, came to visit us, and I cried about what was going to happen to us. She told Papa about a beauty school on Fayetteville Street in Durham that was good training work for girls. They accepted students with an eighth grade education, but I was already in the tenth grade. Nevertheless, Papa agreed it was a good idea, and I went to live with Grandmother Martha until Papa moved us into town in a one-horse wagon. When I saw the movie *The Color Purple*, it reminded me of our move from Chatham County into Chapel Hill.

I never wanted to go to beauty school. I wanted to cook and hear people talk about how good my food was, like they did at church when we had homecoming in August. Still, I went to beauty school and then to work at Friendly Beauty Parlor on West Franklin Street in Chapel Hill. I worked there for a few months, though I never really liked it.

In late 1945, I met Joe Council, fresh from the army. When he took me home to meet his mother, I found her a very likable person who cooked like me. With her fur coat, turkey- or peacock-feathered wide-brim hats, and high heel shoes, she made me feel something I had never experienced before, especially in the way she talked to her son as if they were the best of friends. She made me realize what it felt like to have a mother around. I could talk to her like I thought I would have been able to talk to my own mother, if she had lived.

To my surprise, Joe's mother had known my mother as a little girl in Wake County and talked about the pretty ruffled blouses Mama had when she came home from college. I began to teach Miss Mary, as I called Joe's mother, to spell and write her name because Joe and I needed her to sign for us so we could get married. Even though Joe was not my sisters' choice for me because they thought he was too old, we were married in 1947.

We stayed with Miss Mary after we were married, until a cooking disaster sent me home to Papa. No matter what I did in Miss Mary's pans, I could never make brown gravy to go over the hamburger patties for supper; it was always gray, and Miss Mary was very unhappy about that. So I went home. Many tears and several days later, Joe came to stay in my family's house with Papa, too.

Times were very hard after the war for everyone. Joe worked at the sawmill, like a lot of other men, but when it rained there was no work and no money. I began work in the dining hall on the University of North Carolina campus, preparing vegetables for the cooks, and as a short order cook at the Carolina Coffee Shop, which is now one of the few restaurants in Chapel Hill that is older than mine.

When I began having my babies — our first child, Norma, was born in 1949 — I could work only until they found out I was pregnant. Between then and 1957, all my other seven children (including twins in 1953) were born in between different jobs. The hardest time in my life was after the twins' birth, because both of them — and I — became sick. For almost a year, my right eye would not close, and people began to call me Mrs. Boe, for the man with a patch over his eye on the Bohemian Beer label.

My cooking continued — at Kappa Sigma fraternity and at St. Anthony Hall, when Charles Kuralt was a student and lived there, and for Professor Hugo Giduz and later his son Roland and his family. Joe's parents opened Bill's Bar-B-Q on Graham Street in Chapel Hill. It was a landmark during the integration era because it served lunches for jailed demonstrators. I worked there, too.

My first job doing family cooking was for a Mrs. Patterson on Wilson Court in Chapel Hill. (All I ever knew her as was "Mrs. Patterson"; at that time, blacks used only the last names of their employers.) Her family drank fresh orange juice every morning for breakfast, and I would take the peels home to dry so we could chew on them in bad weather to sweeten "bad breath." Now I know they probably helped ward off colds, but I didn't know that then. I still keep some over a warm place on the stove.

One day Mrs. Patterson told me to cook some sweet potatoes. She didn't say they were for a pie for dessert, but I just assumed that they were and boiled them. I guessed wrong, however, as she wanted them for the main dinner (though I never knew exactly how she wanted them cooked). When I realized my mistake, I decided to try something—I was never given recipes or a cookbook on my cooking jobs—so I mashed them and then put butter, Karo syrup, canned milk, orange juice, a handful of sugar, and a pinch of salt in them. The thought came to me to squeeze the oranges and put the potato mixture in the orange peel cups, then bake them.

At supper time, I set the table and put the food on, but I was so afraid of what I had done with the sweet potatoes that as they sat down I went to stand at the swinging door to hear if I was going to get fired. But what I heard them say was that the potatoes were soooo good. My heart said, "Yes, yes, yes, Dip." And I've been making up my own recipes and cooking them ever since.

In 1957, I began working with my mother-in-law in a tiny take-out restaurant business. Through this experience, I began sharpening my business skills.

In 1976, I was working at UNC Memorial Hospital when George Tate, who was the first black realtor in town, offered me the opportunity to take over a failing restaurant on Rosemary Street in Chapel Hill. I didn't even have the money to put anything down on the deal until my next pay-

Mama Dip in front of her original restaurant on Rosemary Street in Chapel Hill.

check. I had only $64 to buy enough food from a local grocer to make breakfast the first day that my restaurant opened. On a Saturday evening, around seven o'clock, some of my children and I went in and cleaned nearly all night getting ready for our first day.

Sunday morning I stopped by Fowler's Food Store on Franklin Street to shop for breakfast. I purchased bacon, sausage, eggs, grits, flour, coffee, sugar, salt, catsup, chickens, Crisco, cheese, cornmeal, and trash bags, spending almost all of my money and not realizing that I could not have changed a ten dollar bill if someone had given me one first thing that morning. I don't know how many times we ran out of eggs and bacon. The breakfast trade was good enough that I left for the grocery store to buy food to make lunch, and then I used the money from lunch to buy food for the evening dinner. At the end of the day, my profit counted out to $135, and I was in business! I named my restaurant Dip's Country Kitchen.

Monday was a rather busy day for me—back to Fowler's to purchase Coca-Colas; then back to the restaurant to make pies; then to Durham to apply for a restaurant license.

I went from 18 to 22 seats in the restaurant in a year. Not able to add any more seats, we began a take-out business. By 1985, I was able to rent the space adjoining my restaurant and remodeled to seat 90. Soon the restaurant was equipped with a walk-in refrigerator, two ovens, two steam tables, two fryers, and a dish-washing machine. I started out with a staff of three and now have 15 employees.

Since then, I have not looked back. The name of the restaurant changed—to just Dip's—after a trademark challenge. I've taken business management courses at the University of North Carolina in Chapel Hill and several seminars to improve my management skills. And I've been able to hire several of my children and grandchildren, plus nieces and nephews, to work in the restaurant over the years. In 1998 I purchased the land across the street from the leased property where I had been in business since 1976 and built my own restaurant, which opened early in 1999—with the name Mama Dip's Kitchen—and will be a legacy to my children.

The restaurant menu has changed with the times. We now offer vegetable platters, for example. However, there are still people in the community who are interested in cooking game meat, like rabbit and squirrel. Recently, someone called the restaurant and said that he had caught a raccoon in his garbage can and wanted to know how to cook it.

In addition to operating the restaurant, I make, bottle, and distribute my own special barbecue sauce, as well as dressings. Many local specialty food shops sell these, and we sell them directly from the restaurant as well.

Cooks at work in the restaurant kitchen.

Over the years, my restaurant has had plenty of good press. A few years ago, Garrison Keillor brought his homespun live radio show, *A Prairie Home Companion*, to Chapel Hill and invited me to be one of his guests. Afterward, the entire audience seemed to descend on Dip's, eating up "everything—and then some," as one of my daughters described it.

Craig Claiborne, a food critic for the *New York Times*, has written about the restaurant, and it's been written up in *Southern Living* as well. The restaurant has received notice in US Air's in-flight magazine, and it's been featured in a story in the *Washington Post*. We have also had a lot of good publicity from the local papers—the *Daily Tar Heel*, the *Chapel Hill News*, the Raleigh *News and Observer*, the *Durham Herald-Sun*, and many more. In the autumn of 1998, I appeared on the ABC-TV news show *Good Morning, America*, making pecan pie for Thanksgiving dinner.

Preparing and eating different foods has been a mind and soul experience for me. Over the years I have observed that many important discus-

*Mama Dip preparing
vegetables in the kitchen
of her restaurant.*

sions take place and many important decisions get made at a table over a plate of food. All over the world, each country has its own cuisine, and whatever the agenda, food is always important. Whether it's at a picnic or a fancy dinner, food always brings joy to family, friends, and strangers. The best is sometimes the easiest to make. Southern cooking seems the simplest.

More than 15 years ago, people started asking me to write a cookbook. I even got started on it about 10 years ago. But it was a complicated and time-consuming process—mostly because what I've done all my life is dump cooking. Over the past 10 years, though, I've been writing things down and measuring them so I can know I'm giving out the right information for some good country cooking. Still, you should be mindful of my recipes' origins in the dump cooking style. Feel free to modify and adapt them as you like. Experiment with them. Don't worry if your brown sugar is dark or light, if your mustard is yellow or Dijon, if your seasoned salt is Lawry's or Durkee's. Use what you have. Try it different ways. Use your imagination. Treat the recipes like sewing patterns— stretch or alter them to fit. In my own cooking, I've experimented with different spices, shortening, leavening, flour, and meal and noticed the different results that I got from each in different foods. So I encourage you to stretch your cooking luck, too—but remember to try new recipes with your family first. Most all of my recipes have been prepared and served sometime during the 20 years that I've operated my restaurant on Rosemary Street in Chapel Hill. If it were not for the restaurant, I would not have put this book together. Some desserts came from family reunions but never with a recipe. A little of this and that, and do you like it?

After more than 60 years of doing my own dump cooking, which I've shared with family and friends, this is the first chance I've had to put recipes together for a real cookbook. Sharing my cooking with the community reminds me of bringing my dolls together so many years ago for some old-fashioned mud pies. It's another thing in my life that I can be thankful for—spreading my love and happiness like pumpkin seeds all around.

Breads and Breakfast Dishes

Breads

Breads were part of every meal on the farm. The variety was enormous—from fried cornmeal "dog bread," hushpuppies, cracklin' pone, and pancakes to biscuits, rolls, muffins, ash cake, and quick breads. We spread them with freshly churned butter, molasses, or preserves, and at family meals everyone loved to sop up juice from the cooked peas or beans with biscuits and cornbread. There was always a crowd to cook for on the farm, and learning to judge the right amount of soda to put in bread was a real challenge. No wonder I was so delighted when self-rising flour came out!

In the late 1930s, President Roosevelt started the WPA work and food program. One day I looked up and there came a truck that unloaded big bags of yellow cornmeal and brown flour at our house. Now I know that the brown flour was either whole wheat or rye. We also received cases of peanut butter, cases of Karo syrup, and codliver oil. We all hated the codliver oil, but we had to learn to like the flour and cornmeal. We had never seen any brown flour or yellow cornmeal before that. The corn we raised on the farm, and used to make meal, was white, and our flour was white too. When we started cooking with the whole wheat flour, we ate peanut butter biscuit flapjacks, hobo bread, cheese bread, and fried flour bread, but we never battered our good old country fried chicken in that flour.

Hobo Bread

1 cup chopped dried apples, packed
½ teaspoon baking soda
2 cups boiling water
1 stick butter or margarine, melted
½ cup brown sugar, packed
1 egg, beaten
½ cup milk
2 cups self-rising flour

Put the apples and baking soda in a bowl. Pour the boiling water over them, stir, and cover. Let cool, about 20 to 30 minutes. Stir in the butter, sugar, and egg; mix well. Stir in the milk and then the flour; mix well. The dough should be soft and moist like biscuit dough; if it isn't, add a little more milk. Put in an 8 × 8-inch pan and bake in a 350° oven for 35 to 40 minutes.

Serves 6 to 8.

Everyday Yeast Rolls

Rolls may seem hard to make, but they are worth the time. Once baked, these rolls will stay good for three days in the refrigerator. When making yeast rolls, I don't melt the yeast first — I just sprinkle it in, and it does fine.

6–8 cups bread flour
2 packages dry yeast
2 cups milk
1 tablespoon salt
½ cup vegetable oil
½ cup sugar
3 eggs, beaten

In a mixing bowl, mix 4 cups of the flour with the yeast. Set aside. Pour the milk, salt, oil, and sugar into a pot, stirring to mix, and place over medium heat until warm but not hot (lukewarm). Pour the milk mixture into the flour and yeast and beat until smooth. Add the eggs, stirring hard to mix well (using your hands is best). One cup at a time, add as much of the remaining flour as is needed to form a soft dough. Put the dough on a counter or board and let rise to double its original size. Knead the dough 12 to 15 times, until elastic to the touch, and then roll it out on a floured board to about ½ inch thick and cut with a biscuit cutter. Place the rolls in a lightly greased baking pan and let rise until doubled in size again. Bake for 15 to 20 minutes.

Makes 5 dozen rolls or 3 dozen rolls and a 12- to 14-inch cinnamon roll (see recipe below).

Cinnamon Roll

Make dough for yeast rolls as in the preceding recipe, through the first rising. Then cut off a quarter of the dough and roll it out about ¼ inch thick. Brush with melted butter or margarine. Mix together 3 tablespoons brown sugar and 1 teaspoon cinnamon and sprinkle over the dough. Spread ½ cup pecan pieces and ½ cup chopped raisins evenly over the dough. Roll up the dough, jelly-roll fashion, and then pinch the ends of the roll together with wet fingertips. Cut slits on the top of the roll every 2 inches. Place on a baking sheet and let rise a second time until doubled. Bake at 350° until brown (about 15 to 20 minutes). Slice into individual servings and drizzle with honey or spread with confectioners' sugar glaze.

Note: To make confectioners' sugar glaze, mix ½ cup 10x powdered sugar with 1 to 2 tablespoons water until smooth.

Country Kitchen Bran Muffins

This batter keeps well for several days in the refrigerator, so bake the muffins fresh.

1 cup milk
1½ cups all-bran cereal
¾ stick margarine, melted
1 egg, beaten
¼ cup sugar

2 tablespoons molasses
½ teaspoon baking soda
1¼ cups self-rising flour
1 cup chopped raisins

Preheat oven to 375°. In a bowl, pour the milk over the bran cereal and let soak for 20 minutes. Add the margarine, egg, sugar, and molasses. Mix well. Add the baking soda to the flour and mix with the liquid ingredients. Stir in the raisins. Spoon into greased muffin tins and bake for 25 minutes.

Makes 12.

Potato Pone Bread

My uncle would smack his lips on this bread. Rum and raisins are added to make it a good coffee cake. You can buy the minibottles of rum at the liquor store.

2 cups cooked, mashed sweet
   potatoes
¾ stick butter or margarine,
   melted
½ cup dark brown sugar
¼ cup molasses
1 cup buttermilk

2 eggs, beaten
1 cup self-rising cornmeal
1 cup self-rising flour
1 teaspoon allspice
1 teaspoon vanilla
½ cup raisins
1 minibottle dark rum (optional)

Preheat oven to 325°. In a bowl, mix together the potatoes, butter, and brown sugar. Add the molasses, buttermilk, and eggs. Mix well. Mix together the cornmeal, flour, and allspice and combine with the potato mixture. Add the vanilla, raisins, and rum, mixing well. Pour the batter into a 9 × 9-inch baking pan. Bake for 1 hour or until brown.

Serves 12.

Hushpuppies

This fried cornbread is good with barbecue or fish. When frying hushpuppies, don't overcrowd them, or they will cook too slow and be greasy.

1 cup self-rising cornmeal	1 egg, beaten
½ cup self-rising flour	¾ cup buttermilk
2 tablespoons finely chopped onions	

Mix together the cornmeal, flour, and onions. Stir in the egg and buttermilk. Let the mixture sit for 3 to 5 minutes, then stir again so the dough will hold together better while cooking. Drop the batter by tablespoon into a deep fat fryer at 350° and fry until brown all over. Or cook the hushpuppies in a frying pan filled with enough oil to allow them to float. Drain on a paper towel.

Makes about 15, according to size desired.

Fried Dog Bread or Patties

When I was growing up, dog bread was served with greens and creek fish. In the wintertime, when scraps from the dinner table got scarce, this bread was baked in a big, thick pone, then broken into pieces and mixed with milk for the hunting dogs.

1 cup plain cornmeal
1 cup water
1 tablespoon vegetable oil

Stir the water into the cornmeal until well mixed. Heat the oil in a 6- to 8-inch skillet over medium heat just until hot. Pour in the cornmeal mixture and let cook until it appears to be brown. Lay a plate on top of the skillet and turn the bread out onto the plate. Slide the bread back into the skillet and turn the heat to low. Let cook for 10 to 12 minutes. Break into pieces and serve.

For patties, add a little water to the cornmeal mixture if necessary and spoon 2 tablespoonsful of the mixture into the hot skillet for each patty. Let brown on both sides. Makes about 6 2-inch patties.

Biscuits

2 cups self-rising flour
¼ cup lard or shortening
1 cup buttermilk

Preheat oven to 400°. Put the flour in a bowl. With your fingertips, work the shortening into the flour until well blended and evenly mixed. Pour in the buttermilk and mix until a dough is formed. Roll out the dough to about ½-inch thickness on a floured board; cut with a

2-inch biscuit cutter or pluck off balls, roll, and flatten them with your knuckles. Bake on a greased baking sheet for 10 to 12 minutes or until brown.

Makes 10 to 12.

Old-Fashioned Soda Biscuits

2¼ cups all-purpose flour
½ teaspoon baking soda

5 tablespoons shortening
1 cup buttermilk

Add the baking soda to the bowl along with the flour and then mix, shape, and bake biscuits as in the preceding recipe.

Makes 12.

Sweet Potato Biscuits

2 cups cooked, mashed sweet
potatoes
1 stick butter, melted
1¼ cups milk

4 cups self-rising flour
pinch baking soda
3 tablespoons sugar

Mix together the sweet potatoes, butter, and milk until well blended. Stir in the flour, baking soda, and sugar. Shape the dough into a ball and knead about 8 to 10 times on a well-floured board. Roll the dough out 1 inch thick and cut with a 2-inch biscuit cutter. Bake in a greased baking pan in a 400° oven for 15 to 20 minutes or until brown.

Makes about 15.

Sweet Potato Bread

2 cups self-rising flour
½ teaspoon baking soda
1 teaspoon cinnamon
1 stick margarine, melted
1 cup cooked, mashed sweet
  potatoes

⅓ cup orange juice
½ cup milk
1 egg, beaten
1 cup chopped dates
½ cup chopped nuts

Preheat oven to 375°. In a bowl, combine the margarine, sweet potatoes, milk, orange juice, and egg. Mix well. Sift the dry ingredients together and stir them into the sweet potato mixture. Fold in the dates and nuts, mixing well. Bake in a greased 8 × 8-inch pan for 30 to 40 minutes.

Serves 6 to 8.

Cocoa Bread

Stewed yard peaches or apples were served with this bread.

1 stick butter or margarine, melted
½ cup molasses
½ cup sugar
1 cup boiling water
2 cups self-rising flour

½ teaspoon baking soda
¼ cup cocoa
1 teaspoon cinnamon
2 eggs, beaten

Preheat oven to 350°. Put the butter, molasses, and sugar in a bowl. Pour in the boiling water and stir. Sift together the dry ingredients. When the mixture in the bowl is cool, add the dry ingredients, along with the eggs. Stir until smooth. Pour the batter into a greased 8 × 8-inch baking pan and bake for about 1 hour.

Serves 6 to 8.

Banana Nut Bread

1 cup sugar
½ cup butter or margarine
2 eggs, beaten
1 tablespoon frozen orange juice,
    undiluted

3 ripe bananas, mashed
½ cup walnut pieces
¼ teaspoon baking soda
2 cups self-rising flour

Preheat oven to 350°. Cream the sugar and butter together. Add the eggs and beat well with a wooden spoon or for 3 minutes with an electric mixer. Stir in the orange juice, bananas, and walnuts. Add the baking soda to the flour and blend well, then stir into the wet ingredients. Bake in a greased 5 × 9 × 5-inch loaf pan for 1 hour or until done.

Makes 1 loaf.

Crackling Cornbread

This bread was sopped with molasses or eaten with buttermilk.

2 cups cornmeal
1 teaspoon salt
1 cup cracklings
  (see recipe, p. 107)

1 cup warm water or enough to
  make soft dough
1 tablespoon oil

Mix all the ingredients except the oil in a bowl. Heat the oil in a
cast-iron skillet over medium heat. Pour the batter into the skillet,
reducing the heat to low. Let cook for 12 to 15 minutes, until brown.
Place a plate over the skillet and turn the skillet over to release the
bread. Return the bread to the skillet to cook the other side over low
heat for 15 minutes more, until well browned. Or the bread can be
baked for about 35 minutes in the oven at 375° instead. Cut in wedges
to serve.

Serves 6 to 8.

Crackling Bread Pones

2 cups self-rising cornmeal
1 cup self-rising flour
1½ cups cracklings, crumbled
   (see recipe, p. 107)

1¼ cups buttermilk
oil for frying

Mix the cornmeal and flour together. Mix in the buttermilk, then add the cracklings and stir to mix well. Heat the frying pan over medium heat. Add the oil to the pan and spoon in 3 tablespoons of the batter to make a pone. Cook until brown and turn to brown the other side. Repeat until all the pones have been browned. Place the pones in a warm oven until ready to serve (pat with a paper towel to remove excess oil).

Serves 6.

Sunday Cornbread

Cornbread has always been the bread eaten with vegetables and buttermilk.

1 cup self-rising cornmeal
½ cup self-rising flour
2 tablespoons sugar

3 tablespoons butter or margarine
1¼ cups buttermilk
2 eggs, lightly beaten

Preheat oven to 400°. In a bowl, mix together the cornmeal, flour, and sugar. Melt, but do not brown, the butter in an 8 × 8-inch baking pan in the oven. Combine the melted butter, buttermilk, and eggs. Pour them into the dry ingredients and mix well. Spread evenly in the baking pan. Bake for 25 minutes or until brown.

Serves 6.

Cornmeal "Plumb" Bread

*I remember this from visiting my aunt and uncle's house. Beginning
in February, when the supply of the previous summer's canned goods in
the pantry would be getting low, Aunt Laura would bring various side
dishes to the corner of the table to go along with whippoorwill peas or
other entrees. Then she would bring in this dish, made from a recipe that
she had gotten at a quilting party. My uncle said it was "as plumb nearly
nothing as he had ever tasted," but he ate it with coffee year after year.*

2 cups cornmeal
1½ cups boiling water
½ stick butter or margarine
½ cup molasses
1 cup buttermilk

1 teaspoon vanilla
2 eggs, beaten
½ cup self-rising flour
½ teaspoon baking soda

Put the first four ingredients in a bowl and mix them together. Let cool
for about 30 minutes. Stir in the buttermilk, vanilla, and eggs. Mix
together the flour and baking soda and add them to the wet ingredients.
Bake in a greased 10-inch skillet at 325° for 1 hour or until brown.

Serves 6 to 8.

Molasses Bread

3 cups self-rising flour
½ cup sugar
1 stick margarine
2 eggs

½ cup molasses
½ teaspoon baking soda
¾ cup buttermilk

Preheat oven to 350°. Sift the flour and salt together; set aside. Cream
the margarine and sugar and then beat in the eggs. Stir in the molasses.
Dissolve the baking soda in the buttermilk, then add the buttermilk to

the creamed mixture and mix well. Combine with the flour. Pour into an 8 × 8-inch pan and bake for 30 minutes.

Serves about 6.

Breakfast Dishes

Eggs

Eggs were always an important part of country breakfasts on the farm, and we cook eggs of all styles "just right" at Mama Dip's Kitchen. Cookbooks of the sort that reveal the secrets of eggs Benedict rarely tell you the simple essentials of eggs boiled, fried, poached, or scrambled, so I'm sharing them with you here.

Basic Breakfast Eggs

Egg whites: To separate yolks from whites, break the eggs into a bowl and dip out the yolks with your fingertips. Cook the whites as fried eggs.

Soft-boiled eggs: Fill a 1-quart pot half full with water and let it come to a boil. Use a large spoon to put eggs into the water. Boil for 4 minutes.

Hard-boiled eggs: Place eggs in a pot and cover with cold water. Bring to a boil and let boil for 10 minutes.

Poached eggs: Fill a skillet with water and let it come to a slow boil. One at a time, break eggs into a small bowl and pour gently into the water, holding the bowl close to the edge of the skillet. Reduce the heat and cover. Let the eggs stay in the water for 3 to 5 minutes or until they are as firm as you like. Remove them with a slotted spoon or spatula.

Fried eggs: Heat 1 tablespoon oil in a frying pan over low heat. When the pan begins to get hot (after about ½ minute), break eggs into a bowl and pour into the pan, one at a time. For "over light," cook the eggs until the white is just firm, turn them over with a spatula, and immediately remove from the pan. For "over medium," let the eggs cook until all the white is done and the yolk is soft, turn over for about 20 seconds, and remove from the pan. For "over hard," cook the eggs until the yolk is done or break the yolk with the spatula before turning the egg over and cooking for about 20 seconds more.

Eggs sunny-side up: Place a skillet over low heat for 20 to 30 seconds. Add 1 tablespoon bacon fat or oil for 2 eggs. Break the eggs into a bowl, then pour into the skillet. Cover and let cook for 3 to 4 minutes, until the white is firm.

Scrambled eggs: In a bowl, beat 6 eggs until the yolks and whites are well blended. Add 1 tablespoon milk and salt and pepper to taste, mixing well. Heat 3 tablespoons margarine, oil, or bacon fat in a frying pan over medium heat; pour in the egg mixture. Stir lightly with a fork turned bottom up, dragging the fork through the eggs until they are as done as you like them.

Country scrambled eggs: Break eggs into a bowl, but do not beat, and then pour them into a frying pan with oil. Let cook for ½ minute, then rake through the eggs, lightly scrambling, until they are done the way you like them. The eggs should have large pieces of white mixed with soft yellow.

Country Scrambled Eggs with Cheese

6 eggs
½ stick margarine
1 cup grated sharp cheese

½ teaspoon black pepper
½ teaspoon salt or to taste

Crack the eggs into a bowl, leaving them whole. In a frying pan over medium high heat, melt the margarine, but do not let it brown. (Cut the margarine into like-sized pieces before adding to the pan so it melts evenly.) Pour in the eggs. When the whites begin to cook, shake the pan and stir the eggs by raking a fork through them. Do not stir fast. Add the cheese, pepper, and salt. Cook to the doneness you prefer. The eggs should have large pieces of white mixed with soft yellow.

Serves 4 to 5.

Down-Home Hominy and Grits Casserole

Make this for brunch or a covered-dish supper.

1 cup quick-cooking grits
5 cups water
1 teaspoon salt
1 pound sausage, homemade
   (see recipe, p. 110) or packaged
   with extra sage

2 cans (16 ounces each) hominy,
   rinsed
½ teaspoon dried thyme
dash cayenne pepper (optional)
½ cup grated cheddar cheese,
   for topping

Cook the grits in the water with the salt and set aside. Put the sausage in a frying pan and cook over medium heat, using a potato masher to crumble the sausage. Let the sausage cook until just done, then put in the hominy. Stir and cook until the hominy gets good and hot. Drain off the fat. Mix in the cooked grits, the thyme, and—if you like your food a little hot—the cayenne pepper. Put the mixture in a casserole dish and spread the cheese on top. Bake at 350° for 20 minutes.

Serves 8 to 10.

Omelet

This is the basic technique for cooking a plain omelet. Most omelets contain extra ingredients, of course, as in the two recipes that follow this one.

2 eggs
1 teaspoon water

2 teaspoons oil
salt and pepper to taste

Beat the eggs with a fork or beater until well mixed. Add the water, salt, and pepper, beating fast until they are well mixed with the eggs. Heat the oil in a frying pan over medium heat. Add the eggs, turning the heat to low and shaking the pan to keep the eggs from sticking as they cook. When the eggs begin to get firm, fold in half with a spatula, forming an omelet. Let cook until done.

Vegetable Omelet

2 slices onion, chopped
2 slices green pepper, chopped
2 thin slices tomato, chopped
1 mushroom, chopped
1 teaspoon butter or oil for
  cooking vegetables

3 eggs
2 teaspoons water
2 teaspoons oil for cooking
  omelet

In a small pan, sauté the onion, green pepper, tomato, and mushroom in the butter, over low heat, until just tender, about 6 to 8 minutes. Beat the eggs with the water until the whites and yolks are blended together. Put oil in a skillet or frying pan over medium heat. Pour in the eggs and cook as in the basic omelet recipe above, adding the vegetables on top of the eggs and folding the omelet over when it appears to be done on the bottom. Let cook until done on both sides.

Serves 2.

Chicken Liver Omelet

2 chicken livers
salt and pepper to taste
margarine for cooking livers
2 eggs

2 teaspoons water
1 tablespoon oil or bacon fat for
    cooking omelet

Cut the chicken livers into small pieces, put them into a bowl, and sprinkle with salt and pepper. Sauté the livers in a little margarine until done. Set aside. Beat the eggs with the water until well mixed. Heat the oil in a frying pan over medium heat and pour in the eggs. Cook slowly, shaking the pan, and when the eggs are done on the bottom, turn them. Put in the hot livers and fold the eggs over them. Cook until done on both sides.

Serves 2.

Note: Spray the pan with cooking spray before adding the oil or bacon drippings.

Other Breakfast Foods

Pancakes #1

3 cups all-purpose flour
6 teaspoons baking powder
3 eggs, beaten

¼ cup sugar
¼ cup oil
2 cups milk

Mix all the ingredients together. For each pancake, spoon batter onto a hot (350°) griddle or into a greased frying pan over medium heat and cook until the bottom is firm and bubbles break the top surface. Turn and brown the other side.

Makes about 12 to 15.

Pancakes #2

My best pancakes were the ones I made when I was out of regular flour.

3 cups bread flour
7 teaspoons baking powder
3 tablespoons sugar
3 tablespoons oil

3 eggs, beaten
1 teaspoon salt
3 cups milk

Mix all the ingredients together and let sit for 5 to 10 minutes. Stir well. Cook as in the preceding recipe.

Makes about 12 to 15.

Note: To make fruit topping for pancakes, simmer your choice of 1¼ cups frozen fruit (blueberries, sliced apricots, strawberries, peaches, etc.) for 10 to 15 minutes with 2 to 3 tablespoons water and ¼ stick butter or margarine. Add 2 cups maple syrup or pancake syrup. Mix well.

Yellow Cornmeal Flapjacks

1½ cups yellow cornmeal
2 cups self-rising flour
3 teaspoons baking powder
3 tablespoons sugar

1¼ cups milk
2 eggs, beaten
½ cup butter or margarine, melted

Mix the cornmeal, flour, baking powder, and sugar in a bowl and stir in the milk. Add the margarine and eggs. Mix well. Cook as in pancakes #1 recipe above.

Makes about 12.

Cheese Pie

This pie was served most every Sunday morning at breakfast, cut into slices, and topped with gravy.

3 eggs
1 cup milk
½ stick butter or margarine, melted

2 cups self-rising flour
1½ cups aged cheddar cheese, grated

Preheat oven to 400°. Break the eggs into a mixing bowl and beat until well blended. Stir in the milk and butter, then the flour and cheese. Add a little flour if needed to make a soft dough. Place in a large pie plate. Bake for 25 minutes or until brown.

Serves 6.

Coffee Cake

1 box (18¼ ounces) yellow or white cake mix
1 box (3.4 ounces) vanilla instant pudding mix
4 eggs

½ cup vegetable oil
1 cup water
½ cup brown sugar
1 teaspoon cinnamon
1 cup chopped pecans

Preheat oven to 350°. Pour the cake mix into a mixing bowl and beat in the pudding, eggs, oil, and water, as directed on the package, for 5 minutes. Grease and flour a 10-inch tube pan. Pour in about ¾ of the cake batter. Combine the brown sugar, cinnamon, and pecans and sprinkle over the batter in the pan. Add the remaining batter and bake for about 1 hour. Let the cake cool for 15 minutes before taking it out of the pan.

Serves 10 to 12.

Breakfast Chicken

Put these chicken pieces in biscuits and serve for breakfast or brunch.

1 pound chicken breast fillets
(about 4 fillets)
2 cups water for soaking chicken
1 teaspoon salt
¼ teaspoon black pepper

self-rising flour
3 tablespoons vegetable oil
½ cup hot water for simmering
chicken

Soak the chicken fillets for 15 minutes in the water and salt. Rinse, lay on paper towel, and sprinkle with the pepper. Coat the fillets lightly with self-rising flour. Place in a pan and fry in hot oil until lightly browned on both sides. Drain off the oil, add the hot water to the pan, and simmer the chicken for 5 minutes.

Makes enough to fill 12 2-inch biscuits (to serve 4 to 6 people).

Strawberry Jam

2 quarts ripe strawberries, washed, stemmed, and halved
10 cups sugar
½ cup lemon juice

Mix the berries with the sugar. Let stand overnight. Cook over low heat until the sugar dissolves. Then turn up the heat and cook fast for 20 minutes, skimming off foam while cooking. Add the lemon juice and mix. Turn the heat to low and let simmer for 20 minutes more. Store in sterilized jars, following general canning procedures.

Makes 5 half-pints.

Pear Preserves

16 cups peeled, cored, coarsely chopped pears
16 cups sugar
juice of 2 lemons

Mix the ingredients together and let soak overnight. Place in a large pot and cook over low heat, stirring occasionally, for 1½ hours or until the spoon is coated with syrup when removed from the pot. Do not overcook. Store in sterilized jars, following general canning procedures.

Makes 5 pints.

Poultry, Fish, and Seafood

Poultry

Sometimes, when I was growing up, we ate quail or other birds that foraged for seed we had put in and around wire traps set out near the barn. My father also raised a few turkeys, and in one of my less successful cooking experiments, my brother and I fried the first turkey we ever cooked for dinner. Well, why not? We knew fried quail and chicken were wonderful.

The chickens always clucking and scratching about in the yard provided us with fresh eggs as well as meat for the table. And adding chicken feet to gravy made it taste "just right." Fried chicken, chicken pudding, chicken and dumplings—what could be more "country" than these hearty, home-style dishes?

The versatile poultry recipes presented here can easily be adjusted to accommodate special diets: fry your chicken in vegetable oil instead of lard, for example, or substitute low-sodium chicken soup mix for salty bouillon.

Chicken Giblets with Noodles

This was my children's favorite meal growing up. Their souls still long for a good bite of this when they come home, along with hushpuppies.

1 pound chicken necks
½ pound chicken gizzards
1½ quarts water
1 teaspoon salt

1 can (10¾ ounces) condensed
   cream of chicken soup
¾ stick margarine, cut into pieces
8 ounces egg noodles, cooked

Wash and clean the gizzards and necks. Cut them into pieces. Put the gizzards in a pot with the salt and water and let boil 20 minutes over medium heat. Add the necks and let boil another 40 minutes. Skim fat off the top. Add the margarine and noodles and let boil for 10 minutes, adding some hot water if needed. Stir in the cream of chicken soup; mix well. Cover the pot, turn the heat to low, and let simmer for 8 to 10 minutes.

Serves 6 to 8.

Old-Fashioned Chicken Pie

CRUST:
1½ cups all-purpose flour
pinch salt
¼ cup shortening
¼ cup cold water

FILLING:
1 stewing chicken (4 pounds)
3 packets (1.5 ounces each) instant
   chicken broth and soup mix

2 cups broth from the cooked
   chicken
½ stick butter, cut into pieces
3 tablespoons all-purpose flour
1 small can (5 ounces) evaporated
   milk

To make the crust, follow the procedures for pie crust (p. 186). Put the dough in the refrigerator until ready to roll out. Or, use 1 can (10 count) regular biscuits. Remove the biscuits from the can and let them warm to room temperature before rolling or leave the biscuits whole.

Put the chicken in a pot with water to cover. Cook over medium heat until just tender, about 40 minutes. Cool, remove the meat from the bones, and dice.

Skim off the fat and strain the broth; if necessary, add water to make 2 cups liquid. Add the instant soup mix and butter and let come to a boil. Add a little water to the flour to make a paste and stir into the cooking broth, along with the evaporated milk. Mix in the chicken pieces and then pour into a 9 × 13-inch baking dish.

Roll out the crust or biscuits to cover the dish. Place on top of the chicken mixture and cut slits in the top. Or place the whole biscuits on top of the chicken mixture. Bake at 375° until brown, about 45 minutes.

Serves 8 to 10.

Chicken Pot Pie

I use regular canned refrigerated biscuits brushed with butter for the topping of this dish.

1 whole stewing chicken

3 packets (1.5 ounces each) instant chicken broth and soup mix

1 small can (5 ounces) evaporated milk

½ stick butter or margarine, cut into pieces

1 package (10 ounces) frozen peas and carrots, rinsed with cold water

3 tablespoons flour

1 can biscuits (10 count)

Wash the chicken and boil in 1 quart water with the instant broth until tender, about 40 minutes. Remove the chicken, cool, take the meat off the bones, and dice.

Add the evaporated milk, butter, and peas and carrots to the chicken stock. Let cook slowly for about 12 minutes. Thicken the broth with a paste made by combining the flour with a little water. Turn off the heat. Add the diced chicken to the pot, stirring to mix.

Pour the chicken mixture into a 9 × 13-inch baking dish. Pull the biscuits in half and place them over the chicken mixture. Brush the biscuits with melted butter, place the dish in a 375° oven, and bake for 35 to 40 minutes or until brown.

Serves 8 to 10.

Country Fried Chicken

Use a whole fryer, cut up, or parts of your choice. It takes about 2 minutes over medium high heat for oil to get hot enough for frying. If it smokes or pops when the chicken touches it, the oil is too hot.

chicken parts
1½ cups self-rising flour
1 teaspoon black pepper

½ teaspoon salt
1½ cups shortening

In a bowl, mix 2 teaspoons salt with 2 cups water. Put in the chicken parts and let soak for 15 to 20 minutes. Drain. Mix together the flour, pepper, and salt and batter the chicken by dipping the pieces in the flour mixture until they are coated on all sides, shaking off excess flour. In a skillet, over medium heat, let the shortening get hot. It should be at 350° on a thermometer, or you can test it by taking a piece of chicken and letting the corner touch the shortening: if it begins to fry, the shortening is ready. If the shortening appears too hot, remove the skillet from the heat and let it cool a little. Brown the chicken on all sides, reducing the heat if needed as it cooks. It takes about 20 minutes to fry chicken well-done. If you are afraid that the chicken is not done even though the batter is browned, put it in a baking pan and place it in the oven at 350° for 15 minutes.

Serves 4 to 5.

Grandpa's Chicken

Papa often told the story of how Grandpa's chicken was always cooked in a smaller pan. You see, Grandpa's teeth were either scattered or gone, so his chicken had to be soft—but with the fried chicken flavor. If you like soft, mellow, tasty chicken, this is it!

Prepare and fry chicken parts as for country fried chicken, above. When the chicken is done, drain off all the fat. Add 1 cup hot water to the skillet and simmer the chicken, covered, for 5 minutes. Turn off the heat and let the chicken mellow in the skillet for 10 minutes before serving.

Serves 4 to 5.

Barbecue Drumettes

Drumettes are made from the drum part of a chicken wing. Allow 2 or 3 per person.

Prepare sauce as in the following recipe. Soak the drumettes in a bowl of water to which 2 teaspoons salt have been added, drain, and pat dry with a paper towel. Grease a baking pan or spray the pan with cooking spray. Place the drumettes in the pan so that they do not touch. Bake in a 400° oven for 25 minutes and drain off any liquid. Pour or brush the barbecue sauce over the chicken and let cook for 10 minutes more or until just tender.

Oven Barbecue Chicken

Barbecue sauce for chicken doesn't need butter or oil.

1 cup ketchup

2 tablespoons Worcestershire
    sauce

1 teaspoon hot sauce

¼ cup vinegar

2 tablespoons prepared mustard

2 tablespoons sugar

1 teaspoon seasoned salt

1 fryer, cut up into 8 pieces,
    or chicken parts

Wash the chicken and soak it in a bowl with 2 teaspoons of salt added to 2 cups of water. Drain. Preheat oven to 400°. Mix together all of the ingredients except the chicken to make the sauce. Place the chicken pieces in a baking dish. Bake on the lowest rack of the oven for 25 minutes. Remove the liquid from the bottom of the pan, and brush the barbecue sauce over the chicken. Return the chicken to the oven and bake for 20 to 25 minutes longer or until tender (it will be done when the leg feels soft when mashed).

Serves 4 to 5.

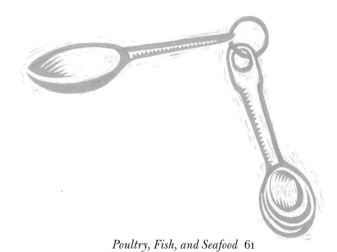

Country Baked Chicken

This has a crispy crust.

1 fryer (3 pounds), cut up,
   or chicken parts
½ stick butter or margarine,
   melted

3 tablespoons self-rising flour
1 teaspoon black pepper
1 cup water

Let the chicken sit in a bowl of cold water with 2 teaspoons of salt for 20 minutes. Drain well and pour the margarine into the bowl, stirring to coat the chicken. Place the chicken in a 9 × 13-inch baking pan, arranged so that the pieces are close together. Mix together the flour and pepper; using a sifter or small strainer, sift them over the chicken. Pour in the water at the edge of the pan. Bake at 375° for about 45 minutes.

Serves 4 to 5.

Note: If too much flour is left on the chicken when it's done, just spoon some of the cooking liquid over the top of the chicken, but remember that this should have a crispy crust.

Mama Dip's Chicken and Dumplings

Around corn-shucking time, an old rooster or hen would be put in a coop to fatten for this old-time favorite.

1 stewing chicken (about 5 pounds)
3 packets (1.5 ounces each)
    instant chicken broth and
    soup mix or 1 can (10½ ounces)
    chicken broth

½ stick butter, cut into pieces
2 cups all-purpose flour
½ cup warm stock
1 bay leaf

Rinse the chicken under cold running water. Put it into a large pot with the bay leaf and cover with water. Let cook over medium heat until tender, about 40 minutes. Remove the chicken and set it aside. When it cools, remove the meat from the bones and chop. Skim the fat off the chicken stock, strain the stock, and return it to the pot, adding water to make 10 cups. Add the instant soup mix or broth and the butter to the stock and heat until the butter melts. Stir to mix.

Take ½ cup of the stock from the pot and add 2 ice cubes to it so that it cools. Put the flour in a bowl and pour in the ½ cup cooled stock. Mix well with a fork or your fingertips to form a dough. Add a little more flour if the dough is too wet. Roll out the dough, on a floured board, thinner than pie crust (not more than ⅛ inch thick). Cut into strips and then into 1-inch pieces. Let the stock come to boil, then drop in pieces of dough. The dumplings will stir themselves in the boiling liquid. When you've finished putting the dumplings in the liquid, shake the pot.

Stir the chopped chicken into the pot, reducing the heat to low. Let cook slowly for 10 minutes.

Serves 8 to 10.

Chicken Pudding

This dish was brought to family reunions by relatives on my mother's side back when I was a little girl. Going down the side of the table of food until I got to the real brown pudding was my favorite thing to do. A hoecake, as called for in the recipe, is just dough pressed out in a pan and baked as a single piece.

1 stewing chicken (5 pounds)
2 cups self-rising flour
4 tablespoons shortening
¾ cup milk
3 packets (1.5 ounces each) instant
    chicken broth and soup mix

¾ stick butter, cut into pieces
1 teaspoon poultry seasoning
3 eggs, beaten
1 cup cracker crumbs, mixed
    evenly with 1 tablespoon
    melted butter or margarine

Wash the chicken, put it in a pot, and cover with water. Boil until tender, about 40 minutes. When the chicken is done, remove it from the pot and let it cool. Remove the skin and bones, cutting the meat into pieces. Reserve the stock.

While the chicken is cooking, mix the flour and shortening together in a bowl, blending them together with a fork to biscuit dough consistency. Add the milk and mix well (the dough may be a little wet). Place all of the dough on a baking sheet and spread it out with your hands to form a hoecake about 10 inches square. Bake at 400° until good and brown, about 25 minutes. Let cool, break into pieces, and place in a bowl.

Strain the reserved stock and measure 9 cups (adding water if needed) into a bowl. Add the instant soup mix and butter, and stir in the poultry seasoning. Cool the broth and then slowly stir in the well-beaten eggs.

Grease a 9 × 13-inch baking dish and line the bottom with the hoecake pieces. Layer the chicken in the dish, pour the liquid over the chicken, and sprinkle the buttered cracker crumbs on top. Bake in a 375° oven for 30 minutes.

Serves 10 to 12.

Chicken and Rice Casserole

1 cup finely chopped celery
½ cup finely chopped onion
½ stick butter or margarine
1½ cups chicken broth
3 packets (1.5 ounces each) instant
    chicken broth and soup mix

1 chicken (3 pounds), cooked,
    deboned, and cut into pieces
3 cups cooked rice
2 cups grated cheddar cheese

Sauté the celery and onion in the butter until soft but not brown, about 8 to 10 minutes over low heat. Remove from the heat. Stir in the broth and the instant soup mix. Mix in the chicken, rice, and 1½ cups of the grated cheese. Pour into a 9 × 13-inch baking pan. Sprinkle the remaining cheese on top. Bake at 375° for 30 minutes.

Serves 8.

Sunday Chicken Casserole

It's quick and tasty.

4 chicken breast fillets, cut in half
¾ stick butter or margarine
1 tablespoon flour
1 cup sour cream
¾ cup water

1 teaspoon instant chicken broth
  and soup mix
1 cup sliced mushrooms
1 small box wild rice blend
½ cup grated mozzarella cheese

Cook the rice according to the package directions. While the rice is cooking, wash the chicken fillets, soak them in a little salt and cold water, and then pat them dry with a paper towel. In a frying pan, melt the butter, but do not brown. Place the chicken in the pan and let cook over medium high heat, turning the pieces until they appear to be done, about 10 minutes. Remove the chicken from the pan, stir in the flour, and add the sour cream. Using a wire whisk to remove lumps, stir in the water and instant broth and mix well. Add the mushrooms. Stir and let this sauce simmer for 8 minutes. Spread the cooked rice in the bottom of an 8 × 8-inch baking pan. Put the chicken fillets on top of the rice, then pour the sauce over the rice and chicken. Sprinkle the cheese on top. Bake at 350° for 30 minutes.

Serves 4 to 5.

Country-Style Chicken Chow Mein

You won't believe the flavor!

3 tablespoons oil
½ pound boneless chicken breasts
   (or mixed meat), cut into thin
   strips
1 medium onion, sliced, then cut
   in quarters
1½ cups sliced celery

1 cup grated or thinly sliced
   carrots
2 tablespoons cornstarch
3 tablespoons soy sauce
2 tablespoons molasses
1 cup hot water
4 cups shredded cabbage

In a large pot or electric fry pan, heat the oil until hot. Stir in the chicken. Add the onion, celery, and carrots. Cook, stirring often, for about 10 minutes. Stir in the cornstarch and then the soy sauce, molasses, and water, mixing well. Add the cabbage and mix well. Cover and let cook slowly for 15 to 20 minutes until the vegetables are just tender. Serve on rice.

Serves 6 to 8.

Chicken Salad

Serve on lettuce with pineapple on the side, or serve in pastry shells. It makes good sandwiches, too.

1 chicken (4 pounds), cooked,
   deboned, and chopped
¾ cup sweet pickle relish
½ cup mayonnaise

3 eggs, hard boiled and grated
¾ cup finely chopped celery
½ teaspoon seasoned salt

Mix all ingredients together and refrigerate until ready to serve.

Makes about 1 quart.

Tonya's Spicy Chicken

I use thighs for this dish. Use only parts that you like, or use a whole chicken, cut up in 8 pieces. The soy sauce and garlic salt should make it plenty salty.

12 chicken thighs
¼ cup vegetable or olive oil
½ cup ReaLemon lemon juice
1 teaspoon oregano

1 teaspoon black pepper
½ cup soy sauce
1 teaspoon garlic salt

Soak the chicken in 2 cups cold water with 2 teaspoons salt for 20 minutes. Drain, rinse off, and pat dry with a paper towel. Place tightly in a baking pan (the chicken should cook crowded). Mix all the other ingredients together and pour over the chicken; let sit for 20 minutes. Bake at 400° on a lower oven rack for 45 minutes or until tender. Turn off the oven, cover the pan, and let sit in the oven for 15 minutes. Serve on rice or noodles.

Serves 6 to 8.

Brunswick Stew

*About the end of harvest time, the women would cook this stew outside
in the big, black pot to celebrate a job well done. In the winter, during
hunting season, the stew was made with rabbit or squirrel and ham bone.*

2 pounds pork neck bones

1 chicken (2 pounds), cut up,
   or chicken parts

1 cup chopped onion

3 cups okra

3 cups corn

2 packages (10 ounces each)
   frozen baby lima beans

6 cups finely chopped potatoes

2 cans (16 ounces each) tomatoes,
   chopped, with juice

1 tablespoon seasoned salt

1 teaspoon crushed red pepper

Rinse the neck bones under running water and put them in a large
(1½-gallon) pot. Cover with water. Let come to a boil, then cook for
30 minutes. Put the chicken into the pot, adding water if necessary to
cover. Continue cooking until the chicken is tender, about 45 minutes.
Take out the pork and chicken. Skim off the fat, strain the liquid, and
return it to the pot. Add 1 quart water and all the vegetables and seasonings. Remove the pork and chicken meat from the bones and cut the
chicken meat into pieces. Put the meat back in the pot and let cook
slowly for 1 hour.

Serves 12 to 15.

Fried Chicken Livers

"As crisp and tasty as any I have ever had" is how Craig Claiborne described the chicken livers he ate at Dip's.

1 pound chicken livers
1 teaspoon salt
1 teaspoon black pepper
½ cup oil

½ cup plus 1 tablespoon
   self-rising flour
½ cup water

Wash the chicken livers and cut off all the green and fat spots. Put the livers in a bowl, sprinkle them with the salt and pepper, and mix well. With a knife handle or other blunt object, pound the livers 2 or 3 times. Coat the livers with ½ cup of the self-rising flour. Heat the oil in a skillet over medium high heat, add the livers, and cook on both sides. Pour off the fat, leaving about 1 tablespoon in the pan. Turn the heat to low. Remove the cooked livers and put in 1 tablespoon of flour, stirring until brown. Gradually stir in the water. Put the livers back into the gravy and heat, covered, about 5 minutes. Add some more water if the gravy is too thick. Serve over rice.

Serves 4 to 6.

Chicken-Stuffed Mushrooms

15 large mushrooms, caps
   separated from stems
2 tablespoons butter or margarine
¼ cup finely chopped celery
2 tablespoons finely chopped
   onion

¼ pound boneless chicken breast,
   diced
¼ cup finely chopped mushroom
   stems
2 tablespoons sour cream
garlic salt

Preheat oven to 350°. Melt butter in a skillet and sauté the onion and celery over low heat until tender, about 8 to 10 minutes. Add the chicken pieces and chopped mushroom stems, cooking until the chicken is done, about 10 to 15 minutes. Add the sour cream, stirring to mix well. Cover and turn off the heat. Let the chicken mixture sit for a few minutes to ripen in flavor. Wash the mushroom caps and place in a baking pan. Brush with melted butter and sprinkle with a little garlic salt. Spoon the chicken mixture into the mushrooms and cover with foil. Bake for 15 to 20 minutes. Serve on a warm platter.

Cornish Hen with Rice Stuffing

This recipe seems expensive to make, but it's not too expensive for a special occasion.

4 Cornish hens (about 1 pound each)
vegetable oil

STUFFING:
¾ stick butter or margarine
½ cup finely chopped onion
1 cup finely chopped celery
3 cups cooked rice

Soak the hens in 1 quart cold water with 3 teaspoons salt for 30 minutes. Place the hens breast side down in the water. Take the hens out one at a time and clean the insides. Dry the hens and rub oil on each. Place the hens breast side up in a baking dish or pan. Cover and bake at 300° for 30 minutes.

While the hens are baking, make the stuffing. Melt the butter in a frying pan, add the onion and celery, and cook slowly for 10 minutes. Mix in the rice and heat until warmed through. Remove the hens from the oven and fill with the stuffing. Let them cool a bit first or else hold the legs with a paper towel or tongs while stuffing.

Serves 4.

Country Fried Quail

8 quail

4 or 5 slices of fatback meat

1 teaspoon black pepper

½ cup self-rising flour for coating
  quail

2 teaspoons flour for gravy

1 cup milk

salt to taste

Soak the birds in cold water with 1 tablespoon of salt for 20 minutes. Fry the fatback meat in a cast-iron frying pan over medium heat until brown. Remove the meat, leaving the drippings. Add the black pepper and mix well. Rinse the birds off lightly and coat them all over with flour. Turn the heat to medium high, letting the fat get hot. Place the birds in the pan, browning them on all sides. When the birds are brown, turn the heat to low and let simmer for 20 minutes, until tender, turning to cook evenly. Remove the birds from the pan and make gravy. Pour off all but 1 tablespoon of fat. Add the flour and milk, stirring well, and bring to a boil. Then reduce the heat to simmer for 5 to 6 minutes. Add salt to taste. Spoon the gravy over the birds to serve.

Serves 4 to 6.

Roasted Turkey

To make roasted turkey complete, serve with cornbread dressing and turkey gravy (see the following recipes).

1 turkey (12–14 pounds)

¼ cup oil or margarine

2 tablespoons seasoned salt

2 stalks celery, cut up

2 onions

1 carrot, cut up

1 tablespoon poultry seasoning

If the turkey is frozen, thaw it as directed. Remove the giblets from inside and rinse the turkey under cold water. While the turkey is wet, rub it with the oil and shake on 1 tablespoon of the seasoned salt, inside and out. Let sit for 10 minutes. When this salt dissolves, shake on the other tablespoon. Put the celery, onions, carrot, and poultry seasoning inside the turkey cavity and fill the hole with a ball of aluminum foil. Place the turkey in a roasting pan, add 1 cup water, and cover with foil. Bake at 325° for about 3½ hours or as directed on turkey packaging. Remove the foil and let cook for 30 more minutes to brown. Turn off the oven and let the turkey sit inside for 20 minutes.

To cook the giblets for use in gravy or dressing (see recipes below), wash them, coat them with flour, put them in a pot with a little oil, and brown slowly. Add a celery stalk and a medium onion. Cover with water, let come to a boil, reduce the heat, and simmer until tender, about 1½ hours, or cover with foil and bake in the oven at 300° for about 2 hours.

Serves about 10 to 12.

Turkey Gravy

4 tablespoons vegetable oil	cooked giblets or hard-boiled
3 tablespoons flour	eggs, chopped
4 cups turkey broth, degreased	salt and pepper to taste

Cook the giblets as in the preceding recipe. Put the oil in a pot or skillet over medium heat. Add the flour and cook, stirring until just brown. Stir in the broth. Reduce the heat to low and let simmer until thickened. As the gravy thickens, add the chopped giblets or eggs. Add salt and pepper if needed.

Cornbread Dressing

This dressing can be served with chicken, lamb, or pork, as well as turkey. When it's served with turkey, giblets can be added to the dressing as well as the gravy.

1 stick butter or margarine
1½ cups finely chopped onion
3 cups finely chopped celery
2 batches Sunday cornbread (see recipe, p. 41), crumbled
4 cups bread crumbs (from bread ends or slices toasted dry)

3–4 cups turkey (or chicken) broth
1 tablespoon dried sage
2 tablespoons poultry seasoning
½ teaspoon dried thyme
3 eggs, beaten (optional)

Preheat oven to 400°. Sauté the onion and celery in the butter over medium heat until tender but not brown, about 8 to 10 minutes. In a bowl, mix the sautéed vegetables together with the cornbread, bread crumbs, poultry seasoning, sage, thyme, broth, and—if you'd like a richer dressing—the eggs. Spread evenly in a baking pan. Bake for about 30 to 40 minutes.

Serves 12.

Barbecue Turkey

1 turkey (12–14 pounds)
¼ cup vinegar
3 tablespoons brown sugar
½ cup Heinz 57 sauce

1 tablespoon prepared mustard
1 cup ketchup
2 tablespoons molasses

Prepare and cook the turkey as in the recipe for roasted turkey, above, up to the last hour of baking time. Mix the other ingredients together to make a barbecue sauce. During the last hour of roasting, baste the turkey frequently with the sauce, omitting the use of foil.

Serves about 12 to 15.

After-the-Holiday Creamed Turkey

Here's a delicious way to use up the last of your Christmas or Thanksgiving turkey.

¾ stick butter or margarine
¼ cup flour
4 cups turkey broth
1 small can (5 ounces) evaporated
  milk

1 can (10¾ ounces) condensed
  cream of mushroom soup
3 cups diced turkey
3 hard-boiled eggs, grated

Once the meat is off the bones of the turkey, make a broth by boiling the bones in 2 quarts of water for 30 minutes. Remove the bones and strain.

Over medium heat, melt the butter in a pot. Do not brown. Stir in the flour, then the broth, milk, and soup. Cook until thickened. Add the turkey and eggs. Let simmer for 15 to 20 minutes. Serve on toast or over rice.

Serves about 8.

Turkey Loaf

2 pounds ground turkey
2 cups bread crumbs
2 eggs, beaten
1 can (10¾ ounces) condensed
    cream of chicken soup

SAUCE:
1 cup evaporated milk
1 can (10¾ ounces) cream of
    mushroom soup
1 small can (8½ ounces) green
    peas, drained

Preheat oven to 375°. In bowl, mix together all of the loaf ingredients until well combined. Put into a baking dish or loaf pan. Bake for 35 to 40 minutes. Turn off the oven and let the loaf sit inside for 20 minutes. Drain off the fat and slice.

To make the sauce, mix the milk and soup in a small pot. Stirring constantly, cook over medium heat until hot. Add the peas and pour over the sliced loaf.

Serves about 6 to 8.

Turkey Noodle Casserole

1 package (8 ounces) noodles
4 cups cooked, cubed turkey
1 can (10¾ ounces) condensed
    cream of mushroom soup
½ stick butter or margarine,
    melted

2 cups milk
1 cup sharp cheddar cheese,
    grated
1 cup bread crumbs, mixed evenly
    with 2 tablespoons melted
    butter or margarine

Cook the noodles according to package directions. Drain. Mix them together with the other ingredients, except the bread crumbs. Pour into a baking dish and sprinkle the bread crumbs evenly over the top. Bake at 400° for 30 minutes.

Serves 6 to 8.

Turkey Lasagna

2 tablespoons vegetable oil
1 pound ground turkey
½ cup chopped spring onion
1 teaspoon seasoned salt
1¼ cups creamed or small-curd
    cottage cheese
1 package (10 ounces) frozen
    chopped spinach, well drained
    or squeezed

1 jar (16 ounces) meatless
    spaghetti sauce
1 box (8 ounces) lasagna noodles
1 package (4 ounces) grated or
    shredded Monterey Jack cheese
    or 4-cheese blend

In a skillet, over medium heat, cook the turkey and onion in the oil for about 10 minutes, stirring and crumbling the turkey while cooking. The turkey should be done but not browned. Drain off the fat, add the seasoned salt, and let the turkey mixture cool. Add the spinach and cottage cheese. Mix well. Cook the lasagna noodles according to package directions. In a 9 × 13-inch baking dish, put the lasagna together in layers, beginning with the noodles. Spread sauce, grated cheese, and turkey mixture on top of the noodles. Repeat to make 3 or 4 layers, ending with sauce on top. Save some grated cheese to sprinkle over the top layer. Bake at 350° for 35 minutes. Let sit for 20 minutes before serving.

Serves 8.

Turkey Roll-Ups

1½ pounds ground turkey
4 cans (4 ounces each) green
   chilis, drained
1 package (10 ounces) frozen
   spinach, cooked and drained

1 can (10¾ ounces) condensed
   cream of mushroom soup
4 ounces Monterey Jack cheese,
   grated
12 10-inch flour tortillas

Cook the turkey in a pan until done. Combine the cooked turkey with
the chilis, spinach, soup, and cheese, mixing well. Spread the mixture
evenly over the tortillas and roll each tortilla up, using a toothpick to
seal it. Bake at 375° for about 25 minutes. Serve hot.

Serves 8 to 10.

Fish and Seafood

Today, thanks to refrigerated air freight, people all across the country
can buy fresh seafood in their local stores. Back when I was growing
up, however, the variety of fresh seafood that was available was limited.
Most of the fresh fish we ate came from the local river, lakes, and ponds.
I remember when the large catfish we used to catch in the Haw River
had to be boiled for 10 minutes, skinned, before it was battered and
fried in lard. I still like fresh fish, battered and fried, but nowadays I buy
sweet, tender, farm-raised catfish — much better and easier — and fry it
in vegetable oil. Many of my fish and seafood recipes use convenient,
economical, canned products, such as salmon, tuna, or crabmeat, and
several recipes feature shrimp, which is particularly plentiful in North
Carolina.

Dip's Barbecue Scallops on Rice

I like extra Cajun seasoning in this dish.

2 pounds medium scallops
½ cup water
¼ cup vegetable oil or 1 stick
    margarine, melted
1 small can (6 ounces) tomato
    paste
¼ cup vinegar

3 tablespoons soy sauce
1½ teaspoons Cajun seasoning
1 teaspoon garlic salt
½ teaspoon black pepper
1 tablespoon parsley flakes or
    chopped fresh parsley
3 cups cooked rice

Wash the scallops under cold running water. Drain and pat dry with a paper towel. In a large bowl, mix together all of the ingredients except the scallops. Taste for seasonings and adjust if necessary. Add the scallops to the bowl and stir so that they are well coated with the sauce. Refrigerate for at least 2 hours. Preheat oven to 450°. Spread the scallops evenly in a 9 × 13-inch baking pan. Bake on the top rack of the oven for 15 minutes. Turn off the oven and stir the scallops, but leave the dish in the oven to let the flavor ripen for 10 to 15 minutes. Serve over rice.

Serves 6.

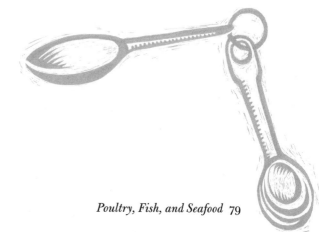

Seafood for Pastry Shells or Stuffed Cherry Tomatoes

1 pound imitation crabmeat, chopped

2 small cans (4 ounces each) salad shrimp, chopped

3 tablespoons grated Parmesan cheese

1 teaspoon seasoned salt

2 teaspoons Dijon mustard

1 teaspoon chopped spring onion

2 tablespoons chopped fresh parsley

few drops Tabasco sauce

black pepper (optional)

pastry shells or cherry tomatoes

Mix all ingredients together and chill until you are ready to fill the pastry shells or tomatoes. Or serve with sesame crackers.

Makes enough to fill 15 small pastry shells or 20 to 25 cherry tomatoes.

Seafood Pasta Salad

The best-ever seafood salad; you will want to fix this for a crowd.

8 ounces small rotini (corkscrew) noodles, cooked according to package directions and rinsed

¼ cup shredded carrots

1 medium zucchini, sliced thin and cut up

2 small yellow summer squash, sliced thin and cut up

2 cups broccoli florets

1 medium red bell pepper, seeded and sliced into strips and cut up

16 ounces imitation crabmeat

3 slices purple onion, cut into quarters

½ teaspoon dried dill

1 cup mayonnaise

1 package Italian dressing mix

salt to taste

In a large bowl, mix together all of the ingredients until well combined. Refrigerate for 2 to 3 hours before serving.

Serves 8.

Shrimp on Rice

1½ pounds medium shrimp, peeled and deveined
1 stick butter or margarine
2 teaspoons garlic salt
½ teaspoon black pepper
2 cups fresh mushrooms, sliced
2 tablespoons Worcestershire sauce
1 tablespoon parsley flakes
3 cups cooked rice

Melt the butter in a saucepan, but do not brown. Add the Worcestershire sauce. Mix in the garlic salt and pepper. Put in the shrimp and mushrooms. Cook, stirring, over medium heat for about 8 minutes. The shrimp should begin to turn pink. Stir to mix and add the parsley flakes. Turn off the heat, cover, and let sit for 4 to 5 minutes. Serve over rice.

Serves 6.

Creole Shrimp

1 cup chopped celery
1 small green pepper, chopped
¼ cup chopped onion
1 teaspoon oregano
3 tablespoons oil or margarine
1 can (10¾ ounces) condensed
  tomato soup

1 tablespoon flour or cornstarch
  (optional)
1 can (16 ounces) tomatoes,
  chopped, with juice
1 pound shrimp, cooked as for
  shrimp salad, below

Stirring often, sauté the celery, green pepper, and onion in the oil over medium heat until tender, about 8 to 10 minutes. Do not brown. Stir in the oregano and then the flour or cornstarch if you want a thicker sauce. Add the tomatoes, with their juice. Add the soup, stirring to mix well, and cook until hot. Let simmer for 10 to 15 minutes. Add the shrimp, stirring to mix well. Cover the pot, turn off the heat, and let the flavor ripen for 10 minutes. Serve over rice.

Serves 6.

Shrimp Salad

You can add 2 cups cooked noodles or macaroni to this to make a more filling meal. Serve on lettuce; or, to serve as finger food for a party, stuff into tomato cups, cucumbers, or small tart shells.

1 pound medium shrimp
½ teaspoon lemon pepper
¼ cup finely chopped celery
¼ cup sweet pickle relish

½ teaspoon horseradish
¼ cup mayonnaise
3 hard-boiled eggs, grated
salt to taste

Peel and devein the shrimp, before or after cooking, as you prefer. Drop them in boiling water and cook until they turn pink, not more than about 8 minutes. Do not overcook. Drain and rinse with cold water. Drain again, chop coarsely, and mix with the other ingredients. Season to taste.

Serves 4 to 6.

Seafood Chowder

The oysters say, "Don't leave me out, please!"

½ pint oysters, cut up
1 tablespoon butter or margarine
¼ cup salt pork, cut into small strips
3 tablespoons vegetable oil
2 cups thinly sliced potatoes
¼ cup sliced onions, cut into quarters, or coarsely chopped onions

½ teaspoon seasoned salt
½ teaspoon black pepper
¼ pound catfish fillet, cut into strips
3 cups milk
1 can (4 ounces) shrimp
1 can (4 ounces) clams, drained

Sauté the oysters in the butter and set aside. In a separate pot, cook the salt pork in the oil over low heat until well done. Remove the meat. Add the potatoes and onion and cook slowly—do not brown—for about 15 minutes, stirring to cook evenly. Add the salt, pepper, and catfish. Stir. Cook for about 5 minutes, until the catfish is well heated. Heat the milk until just hot and add to the pot and stir. Add the shrimp, clams, and oysters. Simmer for 30 minutes, stirring often. Do not boil.

Serves 6.

Old-Fashioned Salmon Patty Cakes

Salmon was served for breakfast in the country when I was growing up out in Chatham County, sometimes with milk gravy.

1 large can (14¾ ounces) pink
   salmon
½ cup bread crumbs

1 egg, beaten
2 teaspoons finely chopped onion
   (optional)

Remove the bones and dark skin from the salmon, then mix all of the ingredients together. Shape into 4 patties. Pan fry over medium high heat, browning both sides. Serve with milk gravy, if you like.

Note: To make milk gravy, heat 3 tablespoons vegetable oil in a frying pan over medium heat. Add 3 tablespoons flour, mix well, and cook for 2 to 3 minutes until the flour is lightly browned. Stir in 2 cups milk and cook, stirring, until thickened. Add a little milk if the gravy is too thick; season to taste with salt and pepper.

Saturday Night Salmon Casserole

1 package (8 ounces) noodles
1 cup sour cream
1 can (10¾ ounces) condensed
   cream of mushroom soup
2 tablespoons mayonnaise
1 cup milk
1 teaspoon dried dill

2 large cans (14¾ ounces each)
   salmon
1 cup cracker or bread crumbs,
   mixed evenly with 2
   tablespoons melted butter or
   margarine

Cook the noodles according to package directions. Rinse and drain. Spread the noodles evenly in a 2-quart baking dish. In a bowl, mix together the sour cream, soup, mayonnaise, milk, dill, and juice drained from both cans of salmon. Remove the skin and bones from the salmon and break the salmon meat over the noodles. Spoon the liquid mixture over the salmon. Sprinkle the cracker crumbs over the top. Bake at 350° for 30 to 35 minutes.

Serves 6.

Salmon Log

Serve with crisp crackers.

1 large can (14¾ ounces) red salmon
3 tablespoons dill pickle relish
1 package (8 ounces) cream cheese, softened

2 tablespoons chopped spring onion (do not include green tops)
¼ teaspoon dried dill
chopped fresh parsley

Drain the salmon and remove the bones and skin. Put the salmon in a bowl and break it into pieces. Add the other ingredients and mix well. Put in the refrigerator to chill for 1 hour. Shape into a log and sprinkle with parsley.

Tuna and Cheese Casserole

8 ounces egg noodles
1 can (10¾ ounces) condensed
   cream of mushroom soup
1 cup milk
2 cups grated cheddar cheese
1 large can (9 ounces) and 1 small
   can (6 ounces) tuna

1 cup crushed potato chips or 1
   cup bread crumbs, mixed with
   2 tablespoons melted butter or
   margarine

Preheat oven to 375°. Cook the noodles according to package directions; drain and rinse. Mix the soup and milk into the cooked noodles. Stir in the cheese. Break the tuna into pieces and stir lightly into the noodle mixture. Pour into a 1½-quart baking dish. Sprinkle the buttered bread crumbs or crushed potato chips on top. Bake on the lower rack of the oven for 30 minutes.

Serves 6.

Tora's Tuna Salad for Sandwiches

My granddaughter Tora loves tuna sandwiches. No celery, please.

1 can (9 ounces) light tuna
4 hard-boiled eggs, grated
3 tablespoons mayonnaise

¼ cup sweet pickle relish
chopped fresh parsley (optional)

Drain the tuna. In a bowl, mix all of the ingredients together. Refrigerate until you're ready to make sandwiches.

Fried Trout Fillets

trout fillets (allow 6 ounces of fish per person)
vegetable oil for frying
1 cup milk
1 egg, beaten
3 tablespoons hot sauce
3 cups self-rising cornmeal
1 teaspoon paprika
salt to taste

Wash the fish under cold running water. Place skin-side-up on paper towels to soak up excess water. Combine the milk, egg, and hot sauce. Dip the fish in the milk wash, drain, and batter in a mixture of the cornmeal, paprika, and salt. Cook in hot oil in a frying pan over medium heat until brown (about 5 minutes for each side), or deep fry at 400° for 5 to 8 minutes. Pat with paper towels to remove excess oil, but be careful, as trout is a tender fish.

Baked Trout

2 pounds trout fillets
2 medium onions, sliced thin
¼ stick butter or margarine
salt

Wash the fish and place in a shallow baking pan. Sprinkle with a little salt. Spread the onion slices over the fish and dot with the butter. Put the pan on the middle rack of the oven. Turn the oven to broil for 6 to 8 minutes, then turn to 400° for 5 minutes. Turn the heat off and let the fish sit in the oven for 10 minutes. Serve hot.

Serves 4.

Fried Catfish

I use farm-grown catfish when I make this recipe, but it's also good for other freshwater fish, such as crappie, bass, or eel. For frying creek or pond fish, you can substitute bacon fat for part of the oil for a better taste.

whole catfish (6–8 ounces each is
   a good frying size)
2 cups self-rising cornmeal

½ cup self-rising flour
1½ cups shortening or oil

Slit the fish two or three times on each side and place them in a quart of water with 2 tablespoons salt. Let sit for 20 to 30 minutes. When ready to cook, wash the fish under slow, cold, running water and lay them on a paper towel. In a pan, mix together the cornmeal and flour. Heat the shortening in a frying pan over medium heat until just hot. Batter the fish by dipping them in the cornmeal-flour mixture and coating well on both sides, placing each fish in the frying pan as you go. Don't pre-batter the fish, because the meat will soak up too much of the batter and take away the flavor. Fry the fish on both sides until done (about 8 to 10 minutes for each side over medium heat), turning the heat up or down as needed. Serve with tartar sauce (see recipe below).

Tartar Sauce

1 cup mayonnaise
2 tablespoons dill pickle relish
1 tablespoon lemon juice
½ teaspoon salt

1 teaspoon hot sauce
1 small cucumber, finely chopped
black pepper to taste

Mix all the ingredients together well and refrigerate until ready to serve.

Beef, Pork, and Lamb

Beef

Hamburger Casserole

This is my favorite casserole. So quick and so good. I use a potato masher to crumble the beef while it is cooking.

2 pounds ground beef
½ cup finely chopped onion
1 teaspoon seasoned salt
½ cup sour cream

1 tablespoon Worcestershire sauce
1 pound potatoes, cooked and
    mashed
1 cup grated cheddar cheese

Preheat oven to 375°. Prepare the potatoes as in the recipe for mashed potatoes (p. 154), halving the butter and milk. Cook the ground beef and onion over medium heat until the beef is browned and the onion is soft, but do not brown the onion. Drain off the fat. Add the seasoned salt, sour cream, and Worcestershire sauce, stirring to mix well. Press the beef mixture into a 2-quart casserole dish. Spread the mashed potatoes over the meat and then top with the cheese. Bake for 15 to 20 minutes.

Serves 6.

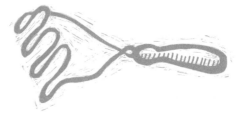

Stef's Spaghetti Sauce

Stefanie is one of my granddaughters. For my children and grand-children, I always serve spaghetti with tossed salad and cooked pinto beans on the side. The kids always mix the beans in with the spaghetti.

1 pound ground beef
½ cup chopped onion
½ cup chopped celery
1 medium green pepper, seeded
   and chopped
1 medium carrot, grated

1 can (16 ounces) tomatoes,
   chopped, with juice
1 bottle (14 ounces) ketchup
2 tablespoons chili powder
1 teaspoon seasoned salt
1 teaspoon garlic salt

Cook the ground beef, onion, celery, carrot, and green pepper in a pot over medium high heat, breaking the meat up as it cooks, until the beef is browned and the vegetables are soft. Drain off the fat. Add all the other ingredients and mix well. Turn the heat to low and let cook slowly, uncovered, for 30 minutes.

Serves 4 to 6.

Buck Mountain Hot Chili Beans

All you need with this is a shake of Parmesan cheese, some hushpuppies, and a glass of cold milk.

1½ pounds lean ground beef
½ cup finely chopped onion
1 tablespoon prepared mustard
2 tablespoons chili powder
2 teaspoons garlic salt
¼ teaspoon cumin

1 teaspoon crushed red pepper
1 can (16 ounces) tomatoes,
   chopped, with juice
2 cans (16 ounces each) pinto
   beans
1 bottle (14 ounces) ketchup

Put the ground beef and onion in a pot and cook over medium high heat, using a potato masher to stir and crumble the meat as it cooks. When the meat is browned and the onion is soft, drain off the fat and add all the other ingredients. Stir to mix well. Turn the heat to low and let simmer, uncovered, stirring now and then, for about 30 to 40 minutes.

Serves 6 to 8.

Meatballs in Salsa

1 pound lean ground beef	2 tablespoons A-1 Sauce
½ pound ground pork	1 tablespoon vinegar
1 egg, beaten	1 tablespoon mustard
½ teaspoon thyme	1 jar (16 ounces) hot salsa
1 teaspoon garlic salt	1 can (8 ounces) tomato sauce

Heat the salsa and tomato sauce together in a small pan over low heat. In a bowl, mix all the other ingredients together well. Form into 1-inch balls. Lightly grease a baking pan or spray it with cooking spray and place the meatballs in the pan. Bake at 350° for 25 minutes. Transfer the meatballs to an ovenproof serving dish, pour the sauce over them, and put the dish in the oven for 10 minutes. Turn off the oven, leaving the dish inside, and let the flavor ripen for 20 to 25 minutes.

Makes about 20.

Hot Dog Chili

Make your hot dog all-American: add mustard, onions, slaw, and chili.

1½ pounds ground beef
½ cup finely chopped onion or 1 tablespoon dried minced onion
1 bottle (14 ounces) ketchup
2 tablespoons chili powder
¼ cup water

In a pot over medium heat, cook the ground beef and onion, stirring and crumbling the meat (I use a potato masher for this), until it is browned and the onion is soft. Drain off the fat and stir in the ketchup and chili powder. Add the water and let simmer for 10 minutes.

Makes about 3 cups.

Sloppy Joes

With chips and Kool-Aid, these make a great Saturday lunch for Little Leaguers.

2–3 pounds ground beef
1 cup finely chopped onion
1 small can (6 ounces) tomato paste
¼ cup ketchup
2 tablespoons Worcestershire sauce
2 tablespoons prepared mustard
2 teaspoons seasoned salt
1 teaspoon chili powder

Cook the ground beef and onion in a frying pan or pot over medium high heat until the beef is browned and the onion is soft. Stir the meat with a potato masher to break it apart as it cooks. Drain off the fat. Add the remaining ingredients, mixing well, and cook until heated through. Serve on hamburger buns.

Serves 8 to 12.

Country Boy Pepper Steak

A poor boy's economy meat dish.

2 tablespoons oil
¼ cup chopped onion
½ medium green pepper, chopped
1 small jar (2 ounces) pimento,
    drained and finely chopped

1½ pounds lean ground beef
1 teaspoon seasoned salt
1 egg, beaten
½ cup bread crumbs

In a saucepan over medium heat, sauté the onion and pepper in the oil until tender. Do not brown. Drain and let cool. In a bowl, combine the cooled vegetables, pimento, ground beef, seasoned salt, egg, and bread crumbs. Mix together well and shape into 6 patties. Coat the patties with flour and cook them in a skillet over medium heat about 4 to 5 minutes for each side. Remove the cooked patties from the skillet and pour out all but 2 tablespoons of the fat. Add 2 tablespoons flour to the fat in the skillet, stirring until brown. Pour in 2 cups water and cook, stirring, until thickened. Put the meat patties back into the skillet with the gravy and cover, turning off the heat after the patties are heated through.

Serves 6.

Stir-Fry Pepper Steak

Serve over rice.

2 tablespoons oil or ½ stick
  margarine
1 teaspoon garlic salt
1 pound round steak, cut into thin
  strips

2 medium green peppers, seeded,
  and cut into strips
1 cup sliced mushrooms, cooked

Put the oil in a skillet, sprinkle in the garlic salt, and place over medium heat until just hot. Add the steak, green peppers, and mushrooms to the skillet. Cook, stirring often, until the meat is cooked as done as you like.

Serves 4.

Stuffed Green Peppers

6 medium green peppers
1 pound lean ground beef
½ cup chopped onions
½ teaspoon garlic salt

1 cup ketchup
1 teaspoon mustard
1 teaspoon seasoned salt
1 cup cooked rice

Preheat oven to 350°. Wash the peppers and cut off the tops. Chop up the tops, discarding the stems. Rinse the insides of the peppers and remove the seeds. In a bowl, mix all the other ingredients together well. Spoon the meat mixture into the peppers. Pour 1 cup water into a baking pan and place the peppers in it. Cover the pan with foil and bake for 45 minutes.

Serves 6.

Beef Stew with Fresh Vegetables

All you need to serve with this stew is cornbread.

2 pounds stew beef
1 cup chopped onions
1 teaspoon seasoned salt
3 cups diced potatoes
2 cups diced carrots

1 stalk celery, cut into ½-inch
  pieces
2 tablespoons flour
black pepper to taste

Rinse the beef under cold running water. Put it in a pot with the seasoned salt and onions. Mix these ingredients and cook over medium heat for about 15 minutes, until the meat is browned on all sides. Add hot water to the pot until it comes to a level 1 inch higher than the meat. Reduce the heat to low and cook slowly, covered, for 1½ hours or until the meat is tender when pierced with a fork. Add the potatoes, carrots, and celery. Cover the pot again and cook, stirring occasionally, for another 20 minutes or until the vegetables are tender. Add a little hot water if necessary to keep the ingredients covered. To thicken the stew, make a paste by combining the flour with ½ cup water (mixing them well) and stir the paste into the ingredients in the pot a little at a time, using only as much as needed to make the stew as thick as you like it. Add pepper and cover the pot and let the stew sit for 15 minutes to ripen in flavor.

Serves 8.

Country-Style Steak

4 cube steaks
1 teaspoon seasoned salt
black pepper to taste
1 cup self-rising flour for coating
   steaks

3 tablespoons oil
1 tablespoon flour for gravy
1½ cups water
dash Kitchen Bouquet browning
   and gravy sauce (optional)

Mix the flour, seasoned salt, and pepper in a bowl. Coat both sides of the cube steaks with the mixture. Let sit for 15 to 20 minutes. Heat the oil in a frying pan over medium high heat. Brown the steaks on both sides, then put them in a baking pan. When all the steaks have been browned, put the water and the tablespoon of flour into the frying pan, mixing well. Add a little Kitchen Bouquet if you like. Pour the gravy over the steaks and bake in the oven at 350° for 1 hour or until tender.

Serves 4.

Meatloaf

A family favorite. Serve with mashed potatoes — a must!

2 pounds ground beef
2 eggs, beaten
½ cup milk
1 cup bread crumbs

1 small onion, finely chopped
½ cup ketchup
1 tablespoon prepared mustard
1 teaspoon seasoned salt

Mix all the ingredients together; place the mixture in a loaf pan or shape into a loaf and place in a baking pan. Bake at 350° for 45 minutes or until firm when pressed in the center.

Serves 8.

Holiday Prime Ribeye Roast

My son William's favorite meal. You can always cook more than you need for just one meal. It keeps a good taste for three or four days and makes great sandwiches.

1 ribeye beef loin (about 6 pounds)   1 tablespoon garlic salt
1 tablespoon seasoned salt   1 teaspoon black pepper

Mix together the seasonings and sprinkle all over the roast. Let sit for 20 to 30 minutes. Put into a baking pan and roast in a 325° oven for 1½ hours. The meat should be cooked medium. Remove the pan from the oven and cover with foil to let the roast ripen for 30 minutes. Place the roast on a platter. For natural gravy, add ¼ cup hot water to the meat juices in the baking pan, stir, pour into a saucepan, and heat.

Serves 6.

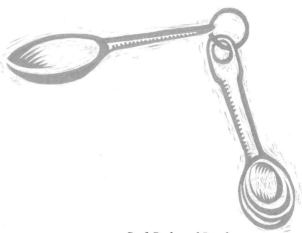

Beef Short Ribs

An old-time favorite.

¼ cup oil
1½ cups self-rising flour
2 teaspoons seasoned salt
1 teaspoon black pepper

5–6 pounds lean beef short ribs
2 cups water
1 cup chopped onions

Heat the oil in a Dutch oven or electric skillet on medium high heat. Mix the flour, salt, and pepper together. Coat the ribs with the flour mixture, then place them in the hot oil and brown on all sides. When all are brown, drain the oil. Add the water and onions to the skillet or Dutch oven, cover tightly, reduce the heat to medium, and let the ribs cook for 2 hours or until tender. Or, after adding the water and onions, cook the ribs in the oven at 325° for 2 hours. Serve on rice.

Serves 6.

Sautéed Liver with Peppers and Onions

My son Roy's favorite meal. This is messy, but it's good. To make liver easy to slice, spread it in a large baking pan and put in the freezer for 20 minutes.

1 pound beef or calf liver, sliced in
    ½-inch strips
½ stick butter or margarine or 3
    tablespoons oil

1 large onion, sliced thin
2 medium green peppers, seeded
    and sliced
black pepper to taste

Put the liver slices in a bowl with 2 cups water and 1 tablespoon salt. Let soak for 5 minutes. Drain well and pat with a paper towel to dry. In a skillet, heat the butter over medium heat. Let the pan get just hot, then put in the onions and peppers. Cook, stirring, for about 3 minutes. Add the liver. Let cook to your desired doneness (I usually cook it about 5 minutes). Sprinkle with black pepper and serve on rice.

Serves 4.

Beef or Calf Liver

When I was growing up in Chatham County, we had only pork liver. It is not as tender as beef liver, but it has a good taste. If you want to substitute pork liver in this recipe, you need to pound it, flattening it out thin, before coating it with flour.

slices of beef or calf liver
   (allow 4 ounces per person)
½ cup self-rising flour
salt and pepper to taste

4 tablespoons oil
2 medium onions, sliced
½ cup hot water

Mix together the flour, salt, and pepper. Coat the liver slices on both sides with the flour mixture. Put the oil in a frying pan over medium high heat and let it get just hot. Place the liver slices in the pan, but do not crowd them. They should brown on both sides. Remove cooked slices and repeat until all the liver is cooked. Pour out the remaining fat and put in the onion slices, separated. Sauté the onions for about 1 minute, then put the cooked liver back into the pan with the onions. Pour in the hot water, stir until heated through, and cover. Turn off the heat and let sit for 10 minutes. Spoon out the liver and onions and serve hot.

Chatham County Corn Shucking Beef Hash

The best hash you will ever eat, this was popular at all corn shuckings. When it was time for a corn shucking on someone's farm, the men would come dressed in their bib overalls, with their shirt sleeves rolled up and their straw hats tilted to the front. Teams of men started at either end of the corn pile, working their way toward the center as they shucked, and there was always a loud laugh when they met in the middle. Some of the men got so tired from the shucking that they couldn't walk straight, and some would later be found asleep in the barn. In preparation for the feast that was part of the corn shucking, some folks would dress a calf and others would buy a hindquarter, wrap it up, and let it down into the well in a tub to keep cool. The woman of the house would be fattening the rooster for weeks beforehand and churning milk for butter, busy with all the preparations. "We will grate these potatoes for her," my aunt would say, "that's been laid in the sun to get sweet." I sometimes fetched the water for cooking and drinking, and I would not want to tote so much water from the spring again, ever.

1 beef shoulder roast (3–4 pounds) or any beef with bone
1 teaspoon salt
1 cup chopped onion
1 teaspoon instant beef broth and seasoning mix
½ stick butter or margarine, cut into pieces
biscuit dough (see recipe, pp. 36–37)

Sprinkle the roast with the salt and let sit for 20 to 30 minutes, then rinse under cold running water. Place in a large pot with the onion. Cover with hot water, let come to boil, and then turn the heat to low and cook the meat slowly until it is very tender, about 2 hours. Add a little hot water if needed to keep the meat covered. Remove the meat from the pot and skim the fat from the surface of the cooking liquid. Remove any fat from the meat and cut the meat into small pieces. Return the meat to pot and add the instant broth and butter. Add hot water as necessary to cover to a level 1 inch over the meat and let simmer. While the meat is cooking, make the biscuit dough. Use half for the hash and refrigerate the other half for later use. Roll out the dough as if for pie crust, about ⅛ inch thick. Cut the dough into 1-inch strips and bake at 400° until good and brown, about 12 to 15 minutes. Break the strips into 2-inch pieces and put into the pot with the meat. Shake or stir lightly. Turn off the heat. Let sit for 20 minutes.

Serves 8.

Grilled Barbecue Beef Ribs

If you try to cook barbecued ribs entirely on a grill, the sauce will burn and char. I parboil the ribs first and then grill them over charcoal just long enough to give them a good flavor, drizzling or brushing the sauce over them. This recipes works just as well with pork ribs as it does with beef.

6 pounds beef ribs or 4 pounds pork ribs
¼ cup prepared mustard
¼ cup vinegar

2 tablespoons Worcestershire sauce
1 tablespoon hot sauce

In a large pot, parboil the ribs for about 45 to 60 minutes, until tender. In a bowl, combine the remaining ingredients to make a barbecue sauce. Cook the ribs on a grill, basting them with the sauce and turning them to cook on both sides, well coated with sauce, for about 15 minutes.

Beef Pot Roast with Vegetables

Leftover pot roast is always good for a pot of soup.

1 chuck roast (3–4 pounds)
¼ cup self-rising flour
2 teaspoons seasoned salt
1 teaspoon black pepper
3 tablespoons oil or shortening
3 cups hot water, as needed

2 medium onions, chopped
3 carrots, cut into ½-inch pieces
1 stalk celery, cut into ½-inch
   pieces
6 potatoes, cut up

Heat the oil in a pot or Dutch oven big enough to hold the roast. Mix the flour, seasoned salt, and pepper together. Place the roast in the flour mixture and turn and rub it until it is coated all over. Place the roast in the pot over medium heat and brown on both sides. Add the remaining flour mixture to the pot, along with 2 cups hot water and the onions. Let come to a boil, then reduce the heat to low and cover the pot. Let simmer for 1½ hours, adding as much of the remaining hot water as may be needed to keep the roast from cooking dry. Add the carrots, celery, and potatoes to the pot and let simmer until tender, about 30 minutes. Or add the vegetables to the pot and cook in the oven at 325°, with the pot covered, for about 1½ hours or until tender.

Serves 8.

Beef Vegetable Soup

A good way to use leftover roast.

2 pounds beef ribs (or use leftover
    beef roast)
½ cup macaroni, or spaghetti
    broken into small pieces
1 package (10 ounces) frozen lima
    beans and corn (succotash)
2 cans (16 ounces each) tomatoes,
    chopped, with juice

1 cup sliced carrots
1 cup diced celery
1 cup potatoes cut in 1-inch pieces
2 cups shredded cabbage
1 tablespoon seasoned salt

Put the beef ribs in a large pot, cover with water, and simmer for 1½ hours, until tender. Remove the ribs from the pot, let them cool, and then pull the meat off the bones and chop it up. Skim the fat off the cooking liquid. Strain the liquid and pour it back into the pot, adding water, if needed, to make 1½ quarts of stock. Put the chopped meat, macaroni, and vegetables into the strained stock. Mix in seasoned salt. Let come to a boil, then turn the heat to low and cook for about 1 hour.

Makes about 3 quarts.

Pork

When I was growing up, we ate pork for breakfast and used it for seasoning fresh vegetables and dried beans. We ate pork more than any other meat. We made sausage and stuffed it in small intestines and hung it up to dry (these are not called link sausages). The ham and the shoulder that had been cured made the redeye gravy that we would have on the table for breakfast. We always had pigs in the pen on the farm.

Most of the fat can be trimmed from fresh pork that you buy now at the market. The fat is on the edge of the meat, which is different from beef, which has fat all through the meat.

Hickory Mountain Hog Hashlet

In Chatham County, at hog killing time, the hog liver, lites, and heart made a onetime meal that many people enjoyed. I don't know why it has the name "Hashlets," but I guess it's because of the way you cook them all into pieces. Lites are the pig's lungs—don't expect to find any in the grocery store.

1 hog liver, lite (or lung), and heart
2 onions, chopped
1 tablespoon dried sage
1 tablespoon salt
2 teaspoons crushed red pepper

Cut the liver, lite, and heart into 2-inch chunks. Place them in a bowl, cover with cold water, and add 3 tablespoons salt. Stir, then refrigerate all night. Pour off the water and rinse the chunks with cold water. Place the meat in a pot, add the seasonings, and cover with water to a level about 2 inches over the meat. Place over medium high heat and boil for about 30 minutes. Turn the heat to low and let simmer for 1 hour, until real tender. Add a little water if needed. The stock should be like gravy. Serve with hot biscuits.

Servings: to each his own.

Lard and Cracklings

Lard is almost forgotten today.

Ask the butcher at the store for fat from pork loins. It should be firm fat, about 3 to 4 pounds of it. Cut the fat into ½-inch cubes and place them in a large pot. Cook slowly over low heat so that the fat won't stick to the pot. Stir often—it will take a while. When the fat begins to get real hot, it will turn brown. Stir so that the fat will brown evenly. When all of the fat is brown or appears to be dry, take the cracklings (the solid, crispy residue) out of the pot and put them in a colander to drain. Let the lard (the rendered fat) sit in the pot so the crumbs settle to the bottom. Put the lard through a strainer to remove the crumbs and refrigerate the lard until ready to use. Use the cracklings for crackling cornbread.

Country-Style Pork Chops in Gravy

6 center-cut pork chops, about ½
   inch thick
1½ cups self-rising flour
1 teaspoon salt

½ teaspoon black pepper
½ cup oil or shortening
2 tablespoons flour for gravy
3 cups hot water

Rinse the pork chops under cold running water. Place on a paper towel to drain. Mix together the flour, salt, and pepper. Coat the chops lightly with the flour mixture. In a large skillet or electric frying pan, heat the oil over medium high heat until hot. Put in the pork chops and let them brown on both sides. They should cook fast enough to brown over medium high heat — about 4 minutes per side — but turn the heat up or down as needed. Remove the cooked chops from the skillet. To make the gravy, drain all but 2 tablespoons of the oil from the skillet and stir in the flour. Mix well and let brown. Stir in the hot water. Return the chops to the pan, reduce the heat, and simmer, covered, for 6 to 8 minutes.

Serves 4 to 6.

Pan-Grilled Pork Chops

4 center-cut pork chops, about 1
   inch thick
1 teaspoon dried thyme

1 teaspoon salt
1 tablespoon oil

Sprinkle the thyme and salt on both sides of the chops. Let sit for about 30 minutes. Spread the oil over the bottom of a large iron skillet over medium heat. Place the chops in the pan and cook slowly, lowering the heat if necessary. Cook 4 to 5 minutes on each side. Cover, turn off the heat, and let chops sit for 8 to 10 minutes.

Serves 4.

Pork Spare Ribs with Sauerkraut

A good cold-day supper, this can be served right from the pan. When buying pork ribs, ask for ribs size "3 and down" (meaning the weight of the whole rib side is under 3 pounds), which are from very small pigs. Large ribs, about 1 inch wide, come from bigger pigs. They take longer to cook and have a stronger taste.

4 pounds pork spare ribs	1 teaspoon salt
½ teaspoon crushed red pepper	1 quart sauerkraut, rinsed,
1½ teaspoons dried thyme	or 2 cans (16 ounces each)
1¼ teaspoons dried sage	6 small sweet potatoes

Cut the ribs apart between the bones and trim the fat. Place the ribs in a pot with water to cover. Add the red pepper, thyme, sage, and salt. Let cook over medium heat, partly covered, for 1 hour or until tender. Remove the ribs from the pot and place them in a baking pan. Skim the fat from the cooking liquid. Strain the liquid, then pour about 2 cups of it back into the pot and add the sauerkraut. Let the sauerkraut cook slowly, simmering over low heat, for 30 minutes.

Preheat oven to 400°. Put the ribs in the oven, first sprinkling a little flour over them, if you like, to make them brown. Turn the oven to broil and let the ribs cook on the lower rack for about 10 minutes. Turn the oven down to 350°. Move the ribs to one side of the pan and add the sauerkraut. Cover and let cook for 30 minutes.

Wash the sweet potatoes (but don't peel them) and rub each with a small amount of oil. Bake them for 45 minutes at 350°. Serve in the pan with the ribs and sauerkraut.

Serves 6 to 8.

Spare Ribs and Rabbit

This dish was always served with kraut or creasy greens during the cold winter season.

1 rabbit, cut into pieces	½ teaspoon dried thyme
2 pounds pork spare ribs	1 teaspoon crushed red pepper
½ teaspoon dried sage	2 teaspoons salt

Wash the rabbit well and place in a large pot covered with water. Let come to a boil, then reduce the heat to medium low and cook slowly for 45 minutes. Add the ribs, the seasonings, and 3 cups water. Cover the pot and let come to a boil. Reduce the heat to medium low; cook until all the meat is tender, about 45 minutes.

Serves 6 to 8.

Note: 3 pounds pork neck bones can be substituted for the spare ribs if desired.

Country Sausage

You can use this sausage in the down-home hominy and grits casserole (p. 46).

1 pound ground pork	1 teaspoon salt
1 teaspoon dried sage	¼ teaspoon crushed red pepper
1 teaspoon dried thyme	

Mix all the ingredients together. Let sit in the refrigerator overnight to season through. Shape the sausage into 8 patties and place in a skillet. Brown on both sides over medium heat (about 4 to 5 minutes per side). Add 2 tablespoons water, and turn off the heat.

Fresh Ham

This ham can be served with dressing and gravy. Use leftovers in slices for grilled barbecue sandwiches or in scraps for chopped barbecue.

1 fresh ham (12 pounds)	2 tablespoons self-rising flour
3 teaspoons dried thyme	salt and pepper to taste
2 tablespoons salt	

Put the ham, thyme, and salt in a large pot, cover with hot water, and let simmer for 2 hours. Remove the ham from the pot and let it cool. When the ham is cool, cut off the skin and fat. Mix the salt and pepper with the flour, and sprinkle the ham with the flour mixture. Place the ham in a baking pan and bake at 350° for 40 minutes. Turn off the oven and let the ham sit inside for 20 to 30 minutes. Remove the ham from the pan and pour the juices into a cup or small bowl. Set the cup in cold water to harden the fat; remove the fat when it becomes solid. Slice the ham and serve with its natural juices, or make gravy to go with it.

Serves 12 to 14.

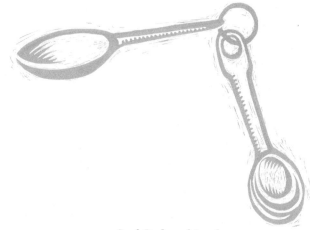

Country Ham

When buying a country ham, make sure that the ham is soft all over when mashed with your thumb and that the skin is not dry and hard. Allow plenty of time to prepare a country ham. It soaks and cooks for a long while. Use leftovers to make sandwiches and biscuits.

1 country ham (12–14 pounds)
½ cup molasses
1 cup brown sugar

GLAZE:
2 tablespoons honey
2 tablespoons prepared mustard
2 tablespoons brown sugar

Scrub the ham with a brush under warm running water and put it in a large pot (the same one it will be cooked in) to soak. Cover the ham with cold water and let soak for 6 hours or overnight. Rinse the ham and then put it back into the pot and put in enough hot water to almost cover the ham. Let the water come to the boiling point, then turn the heat to low. Add the brown sugar and molasses, and let simmer for 3 hours, adding hot water as needed to keep the ham covered. Remove the ham from the pot, let it cool a bit, and then trim off the skin and most of the fat, leaving only a thin layer. Mix together the glaze ingredients and brush them over the ham. Put the ham in a large baking pan and cover with foil. Bake the ham in a 300° oven for 1 hour. Turn the oven off and let the ham stay inside until cool.

Serves about 15.

Ham, Macaroni, and Cheese Casserole

8 ounces macaroni, cooked and
    drained
¼ stick margarine
1 tablespoon flour

2½ cups milk
2 cups grated sharp cheddar
    cheese
2 cups baked ham pieces

Preheat oven to 350°. Melt the margarine in a saucepan. Stir in the
flour until well mixed. Pour in the milk, stirring until thickened. Stir in
1½ cups of the cheese and mix well. Stir the ham into the cheese sauce;
then stir the cheese sauce into the macaroni in a casserole dish. Top
with the remaining cheese. Bake for 30 minutes.

Serves 6 to 8.

Ham and Redeye Gravy

*On the farm, the coffee was always made before the ham or shoulder meat
finished cooking so we could use coffee to make redeye gravy.*

country ham slices
3 tablespoons vegetable oil

¼ cup brewed coffee
¼ cup water

Cut slits in the edges of the ham pieces, so that the ham won't curl up
as it cooks. Place the ham in very warm water and let sit for about 10
minutes, then rinse lightly under cold running water. In a large skillet,
heat the vegetable oil and add as many of the ham pieces as will fit,
cooking over medium high heat. Turn the ham to brown on both sides.
Put the browned ham pieces in a serving dish and keep warm until all
are cooked. When the last of the ham is removed from the skillet, pour
in the coffee and water and let them come to a quick boil. Stir the gravy
and pour over the ham pieces.

Hot Red Beans and Rice

My cousin in Durham brings this to our family reunion every year, always in the cooking pot.

1 pound red beans	1½ teaspoons garlic salt
1 country ham hock	1 teaspoon crushed red pepper
1 medium onion, chopped	1 can (6 ounces) tomato paste

Put the red beans in a bowl and cover them with warm water. Let them soak for 2 hours. Scrub the ham hock in warm water. Put it into a pot with 2 quarts water, bring to a boil, and then cook slowly for an hour. Add the beans, onion, garlic salt, and crushed red pepper to the pot. Cook slowly until the beans are done (see the package for the recommended cooking time). Add a little hot water if needed to keep the ingredients covered. When the beans are done, stir in the tomato paste. Remove the ham hock, chop up the lean meat, and put it back in the pot. Serve on rice.

Serves 6 to 8.

Pork Tenderloin

This is good for breakfast. The water added at the end makes the pork good and tender.

1 pound pork tenderloin	½ teaspoon salt
1 cup self-rising flour	3 tablespoons vegetable oil
1 teaspoon black pepper	½ cup hot water

Wash the meat and dry it with a paper towel. Cut off the fat and then cut the pork into ¼-inch slices. Mix together the flour, pepper, and salt. Coat the meat in the flour mixture. Heat the oil in a skillet over medium high heat and cook the pork slices, a few at a time, until brown on both sides, about 5 to 6 minutes. Pour off the fat. Return the cooked pork slices to the skillet, add the hot water, and cover. Turn off the heat and let sit for 10 minutes.

Serves 4 to 6.

Roast Pork Loin

Ask the butcher to chine and cut away the bone for easy carving.

1 pork loin (8–10 pounds)	1 tablespoon salt
1 teaspoon dried sage	1 cup water
1 tablespoon dried thyme	

Combine the sage, thyme, and salt in a small bowl. Trim any fat from the meat and rinse the loin under cold running water. Place the wet loin in a baking pan and rub it with the mixture of sage, thyme, and salt. Pour the water into the pan. Cover the pan loosely with foil and let sit for 30 minutes. Bake the loin at 400° for 1 hour, then remove the foil and bake for 20 minutes more. Serve with the natural juices, after skimming off the fat.

Serves 10.

Chitlins

Fraternity brothers at the University of North Carolina at Chapel Hill once brought pledges to Dip's and ordered them chitlins, as if chitlins were a downside to fraternity initiation. Invariably the pledges liked the chitlins — if not the concept of eating intestines, then at least their flavor, which depends entirely on proper seasoning and family traditions.

10 pounds pork chitlins
  (chitterlings)
½ tablespoon dried sage

1 teaspoon crushed red pepper
2 tablespoons salt
1 teaspoon dried thyme

Wash the chitlins and remove the excess fat. Place the chitlins in a large pot filled with warm water to a level 3 inches over the chitlins. Add the seasonings. Cook over low heat for 3 hours or until tender. Skim off the fat that comes to the top of the pot as the chitlins cook. Remove the chitlins from the water, chop in small pieces, and serve hot.

Serves 6.

Fried Chitlins

pork chitlins, boiled
1 cup self-rising flour
1 teaspoon black pepper

2 tablespoons oil (or vegetable
  cooking spray to coat skillet)

Coat the chitlins in the flour and pepper mixed together. Place them in the oil in a skillet over medium heat. Cook slowly, about 10 minutes on each side, turning, until crispy and brown all over. Drain on paper towels.

Pig Tails or Neck Bones

3 pounds pig tails or neck bones   1 teaspoon dried thyme
1 teaspoon crushed red pepper   1 tablespoon salt

Wash the pig tails or neck bones and trim off the fat. Place them in a pot and cover with water. Add the seasonings. Let come to a boil. Turn the heat to low and cook slowly until tender, about 1½ hours.

Hog Mall (Maw) with Sauerkraut

The next best thing to chitlins.

5 pounds hog malls (stomachs)   1 teaspoon crushed red pepper
1 teaspoon dried thyme   1 quart sauerkraut or 2 cans
1 teaspoon dried sage   (16 ounces each)

Wash the hog malls and cut away the excess fat. Place the malls in a large pot along with the seasonings and cover with water. Cook slowly for 3 to 3½ hours. Remove the malls from the pot and place them in a baking dish along with 1 cup of the cooking liquid from which the fat has been skimmed. Add the sauerkraut, cover the pan tightly with foil, and bake in a 325° oven for 45 minutes. Add water if needed to keep the malls from drying out.

Servings: to each his own.

Lamb

Lamb Chops

Molasses adds that special flavor.

8 lamb chops, cut thick
  (about 1–1½ inches)
1 teaspoon salt
½ teaspoon black pepper
½ teaspoon dried thyme

½ cup self-rising flour
3 tablespoons vegetable oil
¼ cup water
2 tablespoons molasses

Rinse the lamb chops under cold running water, shaking off the excess water. Sprinkle both sides of the chops with the salt, pepper, and thyme. Let the chops sit for 20 minutes. Place the flour in a pan or dish and dip the chops in the flour to coat on both sides; shake off any excess flour. Heat the oil in a frying pan over medium heat, add the chops, and cover the pan. Let cook on both sides until brown, about 6 to 8 minutes per side. Pour off the excess fat and add the water and molasses. Cover the pan, turn off the heat, and let stand for about 20 minutes so the chops will get moist and tender.

Serves 8.

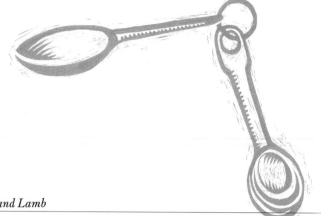

Lamb Shanks or Knuckles

Lamb shanks are cut into four quarters similar to ham hocks. An electric skillet cooks these best, but if you don't have one, you can brown the shanks on top of the stove and then move them into the oven. When shanks are cooking, they can simmer crowded, but don't forget to turn them.

4 lamb shanks	1 teaspoon garlic salt
1 cup self-rising flour	¼ cup oil
1 teaspoon black pepper	2 cups hot water

Combine the flour, pepper, and garlic salt. Coat the lamb shanks all over with the flour mixture. Heat the oil in a skillet over medium high heat and add as many of the shanks as will fit. Cook, turning, until the shanks are browned on all sides, about 20 minutes. Repeat until all the shanks are done.

If you are using an electric skillet, dip out the oil, then return the shanks to the skillet and pour in the water. Cover and cook at 325° for 2 hours or until tender. Transfer the shanks to a serving dish. Remove the excess fat from the juices in the skillet and thicken the juices with 1 tablespoon flour mixed with as little water as needed to make a paste. Stir the paste into the juices and cook for a few minutes until thickened, adding water if necessary to prevent the gravy from becoming too thick. To cook the shanks in the oven, place the browned shanks in a baking pan, pour in the water, and cover the pan with foil. Bake at 325° for 2 hours or until tender. Remove the excess fat from the juices in the baking pan, transfer the juices to a saucepan, and thicken as directed above.

Serves 4.

Leg of Lamb

Serve with your favorite dressing.

1 leg of lamb (about 8 pounds)
1 tablespoon salt
¼ cup vinegar
1 tablespoon garlic salt
1 teaspoon black pepper
½ jar (4 ounces) tomato jam (see
   recipe, p. 166) or apple jelly
2 tablespoons self-rising flour

GRAVY:
pan juices, fat skimmed off
2 cups water
2 tablespoons oil
2 tablespoons all-purpose flour

Trim the fat from the lamb. In a Dutch oven, cover the lamb with water to which you have added the salt and vinegar and soak for 35 minutes. Remove the lamb from the water but do not pat dry. Sprinkle the garlic salt and pepper over the lamb. Place the lamb in a baking pan and cover with foil. Bake for 2 hours in a 325° oven. Remove the lamb from the oven; dip the juices out of the pan, skim off the fat, and reserve the juices for making gravy. Stir the jelly and brush it over the lamb. Using a sifter or small strainer, sift the flour over the lamb. Place the lamb back in the oven, uncovered, turn the heat up to 375°, and let bake for 30 minutes. Turn off the oven and shake some additional garlic salt on the lamb, to taste. Let the lamb stand in the oven about 30 minutes to ripen in flavor.

To make the gravy, add the water to the pan juices. In a saucepan over medium heat, brown the flour in the oil. Stirring all the while, add the pan juices and water. Turn the heat to low and let simmer for 5 minutes, adding water if needed to keep the gravy from getting too thick.

Serves 8 to 10.

Vegetables
and Salads

Vegetables

Vegetables were the mainstays of our meals when I was growing up. Some days there was meat to go along with them; some days there wasn't. Vegetables were grown on the farm or foraged from the fields. Poke salad greens grew wild around the barn. People say pokeweed is poisonous now, but we used it in so many ways—even using the berries to dye petticoats. Creasy salad came wild from the corn and cotton fields. Today, creasy greens can't easily be found because they're killed by the chemical herbicides that farmers use more often in their fields. We planted all sorts of peas—black-eyed, whippoorwill, and crowder—which were dried or just canned in glass jars. Our family grew and popped popcorn, but field corn was just as tasty roasted up brown and crunchy on the woodstove.

The fresher the vegetables, the better the flavor. To get the freshest possible vegetables for Mama Dip's Kitchen, I buy them directly from the farmers' markets around town. My advice for preparing freshly picked greens is to start by letting them sit in salt water for 10 to 15 minutes to upset the insects, if any. Then rinse them three more times in fresh water. Take off any long stems and look for webs on the back of the leaves.

Vegetables cooked country style don't have to be greasy. I have always searched for what will give them the best taste, and I find that lean, cured side meat and ham hocks are still my favorites (rather than fatback) for seasoning cabbage, dried limas, fresh string beans, collard greens, dried peas, and stewed corn. I let the meat simmer until the water turns cloudy. I cook the vegetables with only a small amount of water in the pot, adding a little more hot water as needed to keep them from getting too dry.

Oven-Fried Green Tomatoes

In late summer, when all the vegetables were canned or made into soup, fried tomatoes were always on the breakfast table.

4 green tomatoes, sliced
½ stick butter or margarine
1 teaspoon salt

1 teaspoon black pepper
1 cup self-rising flour

Preheat oven to 400°. Melt the butter in a baking pan. Stir in the salt and pepper. Coat the sliced tomatoes with flour and place them in the pan. Bake on the lower rack of the oven for 8 minutes. Then turn the oven up to broil in order to brown the tomato slices.

Serves about 6.

Spring Vegetable Pot

My favorite.

2 cups fresh shelled green peas
1 pound small new potatoes
6 asparagus spears, cut into
    4 pieces
½ stick butter, cut into pieces

2 tablespoons flour
¼ cup water
1 small can (5 ounces) evaporated
    milk
salt and pepper to taste

Scrape or peel the potatoes. Cook the peas at a slow boil in a quart of water for 30 minutes. Add the potatoes, and add some hot water to the pot if needed to cover the vegetables. Boil for 20 minutes more. Add the asparagus and butter and simmer until the asparagus is tender, about 10 minutes. Add the evaporated milk. Mix together the flour and water and add the paste to the pot a little at a time to thicken the liquid into a cream sauce. Add salt and pepper. Cover and turn off the heat. Let sit for about 10 minutes for the flavor to ripen.

Serves 6.

Pole Beans

These flat beans, usually 5 to 8 inches long and called Kentucky Wonder or Spanish beans, as well as pole beans, have a sweeter flavor than regular green beans. They have strings, which are not as tender as the bean, so be sure to pull them out. Pole beans are best when they are about ½ inch wide and 6 inches long.

2 pounds fresh pole beans
¼ pound country side meat
1½ quarts water

½ teaspoon sugar
1 teaspoon salt

Cut three slits in the side meat and rinse it with warm water. Place it in a pot with the water, sugar, and salt. Bring to a boil. Reduce the heat to low and cook for 45 minutes. Wash the beans, break them into 1- to 2-inch pieces, removing the ends, and add them to the pot. Bring the water to a boil again, then reduce the heat to low and cook the beans slowly, stirring often, for about 35 minutes. Add a little hot water if needed. There should be very little water left in the pot when the beans are done.

Serves 6.

Green Beans

Buy small slender beans that are fresh looking and not withered.

2 pounds fresh green beans
¼ pound country side meat
1½ quarts water

½ teaspoon sugar
1 teaspoon salt

Wash the beans; break off and discard a small piece from each end. Leave the beans whole or break them into pieces the size you like. Follow the cooking procedures for pole beans in the preceding recipe.

Serves 6.

Eggplant Casserole #1

When I first made this dish, I had never seen eggplants before. The family I cooked it for loved it!

2 large eggplants
½ stick butter or margarine,
    melted
½ cup milk
1 can (10¾ ounces) condensed
    cream of mushroom soup

2 eggs, beaten
1 teaspoon salt
¼ teaspoon black pepper
½ cup cracker crumbs, mixed
    evenly with 2 tablespoons
    melted butter or margarine

Peel and slice the eggplant. Put the eggplant slices into a 2-quart pot with water (enough to cover) and 2 teaspoons salt and cook until tender, about 15 minutes. Stir often to cook evenly. Drain. Add the butter, soup, milk, eggs, salt, and pepper, stirring to mix well. Pour into a 1½-quart baking dish. Sprinkle the buttered cracker crumbs over the eggplant mixture. Bake at 375° on the lower rack of the oven for 30 minutes.

Serves 6.

Eggplant Casserole #2

2 medium eggplants
½ stick margarine, cut into pieces
¼ cup milk
1 can (10¾ ounces) condensed
   cream of mushroom soup

2 eggs, beaten
1 teaspoon garlic salt
½ cup Parmesan cheese

Peel and slice the eggplants. Cook them in a small amount of hot water
with 2 teaspoons salt, stirring to cook evenly, until very tender, about
15 minutes. Drain, then mash the eggplant pieces with a potato masher,
adding the margarine as you mash. Add the milk, soup, eggs, garlic salt,
and Parmesan cheese. Mix well. Place in a casserole dish and bake at
400° for 20 to 30 minutes.

Serves 6.

Fresh Stewed Corn

Corn is a year-round favorite that will accompany any vegetable or meat. When cutting corn from the cob, use a sharp knife and make two complete cuts. Cut off the tip of the grain first, then cut or scrape next to the cob. As you cut the corn off the cob, look for and pull out embedded silks.

5–6 ears of corn (white or yellow)
1 tablespoon flour
1 teaspoon salt
1 cup water

2 tablespoons bacon fat, or
½ stick butter or margarine,
or drippings from 2 slices of
fried salt pork

In a bowl, stir the flour, salt, and water into the corn that has been removed from the cob; then place the corn mixture in a pot. Cook over medium heat until the corn gets very hot, stirring 3 or 4 times. Add the fat or margarine. Reduce heat to low and let simmer for 15 minutes, stirring often.

Serves 4 to 6.

Roasted Corn

In July, when the corn began to get ripe enough to eat, "it's roasting ear time," we would say!

Shuck the corn and remove the silks. Wash the corn and dry it with paper towels. Place the ears directly on the middle oven rack. Bake at 375° for 20 minutes. Turn oven to broil and turn corn to brown all over, cooking about 15 minutes more. Serve with butter.

Corn on the Cob with Garlic Parsley Butter

Use yellow or white corn. The ears should be filled out, but not so old that juice will not pop out easily when you mash the kernels with your thumb.

SAUCE:

1 stick melted butter

1 tablespoon garlic salt

1 tablespoon chopped parsley

Shuck the corn and clean out the silks. I use a brush and hold the ear under cold running water while brushing the corn. Cut or break off the tip of the ear. Place the corn in a pot and cover with hot water. Boil for 10 minutes. Remove the pot from the heat and let the corn sit in the water for 10 more minutes.

Remove the corn from the water, drain, and brush the ears with butter sauce, made by combining the ingredients above.

Makes enough sauce to brush on 12 ears of corn.

Note: To cook corn in the microwave, wrap 2 ears in plastic wrap and microwave on high for 5 minutes. To grill corn on the cob, leave a layer of shucks on the ears and heat over charcoal for about 20 minutes, turning occasionally.

Corn and Limas

In the country, many vegetables were cooked together. Serve this with fresh sliced tomatoes and buttered okra.

2 cups lima beans
1 teaspoon salt
½ stick butter or margarine,
   cut into pieces

3 cups fresh corn (yellow or
   white), cut from the cob
1 tablespoon flour
1 teaspoon sugar (optional)

Rinse the limas under cold running water. Place them in a pot and cover with hot water to a level about 1 inch over the beans. Add the salt and butter. Let cook over low heat until tender, about 35 minutes, adding a little hot water if needed. In a bowl, mix the corn with the flour; add them to the limas, along with the sugar, if you like. Simmer for 15 minutes. Add a little hot water if needed, but corn and limas should not be runny. Turn off the heat and cover. Let stand for 15 minutes.

Serves 6.

Old-Fashioned Succotash

We would can cases of mixed vegetables in the summer. In the winter, we would heat them up, adding either butter or redeye gravy left in the bowl from breakfast, and serve them with biscuits. This freezes well for adding to soup later on.

2 cups lima beans
1 teaspoon salt
6 ripe medium tomatoes, peeled, diced, and drained, or 1 can
   (14½ ounces) tomatoes, drained and diced
2 cups cut-up okra, fresh or unthawed frozen
¾ stick butter or margarine, cut into pieces, or 3 tablespoons bacon fat
3 cups fresh white corn, cut from the cob

Wash the limas in cold water. Put them into a 2-quart pot, cover the beans with water, and add salt. Let the limas cook over low heat until tender, about 30 minutes. Add a little water if needed; all of the water should be gone when the limas are cooked. Add the tomatoes, okra, and butter. Stir the corn into the pot. Cook slowly for 15 minutes, then turn off the heat and let stand for 15 to 20 minutes.

Serves 8 to 10.

Fresh Corn Casserole

I prefer to use yellow corn to make this dish, which goes well with baked chicken and barbecue.

3 cups fresh yellow corn, cut from the cob
1 tablespoon flour
½ stick butter or margarine, melted
2 tablespoons brown sugar
1 teaspoon garlic salt
1 tablespoon chopped parsley
1 cup milk
2 eggs, beaten
1 small jar (2 ounces) pimentos, chopped

Preheat oven to 350°. In a bowl, mix the corn kernels with the flour. Add the remaining ingredients and mix well. Pour into a baking dish and bake for 1 hour.

Serves 4 to 6.

Pinto Beans with Corn

Chow-chow goes well with this.

1 pound dry pinto beans
¼ pound country side meat
   or salt pork
2 teaspoons salt

2 packages (10 ounces each)
   frozen corn, or 4 cups fresh
   corn, cut from the cob

Wash the beans by putting them in a large bowl with warm water. Stir them around with your fingers until the water becomes cloudy, then drain. Rinse the beans and drain again. Place the beans in a 2-quart pot and fill with hot water to a level about 3 inches over the beans. Add the side meat and salt. Cover the pot and simmer for 2½ hours or until the beans are tender (stir occasionally, checking to be sure there is enough liquid). Pintos should have a saucelike juice when they are done. Cook a bit longer if necessary for more of the juice to be absorbed. Add the corn and let simmer for 20 minutes. Stir occasionally, adding hot water if needed.

Serves 6 to 8.

Chow-chow

The perfect mate for dried beans. Chop the vegetables fine or coarse,
as you prefer.

3 tablespoons pickling spice
2 tablespoons salt
4 cups water
4 medium red bell peppers,
    seeded and chopped
2 cups chopped onion

1 small cabbage, chopped
2 cups chopped green tomatoes
2 cups vinegar
1 cup sugar
1 hot pepper pod, chopped

Add the pickling spice and salt to the water in a small pot. Bring to
a boil and let boil for 10 minutes. Mix all the remaining ingredients
together in a large pot and add the spiced water, pouring it through a
strainer. Let cook slowly for 35 to 45 minutes, stirring often. Taste for
seasoning. Store in sterile half-pint jars or refrigerate.

Makes about 12 small jars.

Baked Beans

A cookout favorite!

2 cans (16 ounces each)
    pork 'n' beans, drained
1 can (6 ounces) tomato paste
¼ cup finely chopped onion

½ cup ketchup
2 tablespoons molasses
2 tablespoons brown sugar
2 strips bacon

Preheat oven to 400°. Place all of the ingredients, except the bacon, in a
bowl. Stir until well mixed. Pour the beans into a baking pan and lay the
bacon on top. Baked uncovered for 30 to 40 minutes.

Serves 8 to 10.

Great Northern Beans with Tomatoes

This was my children's favorite vegetable dish when they were growing up.

1 pound dried northern beans
7 cups water
¼ pound salt pork or country
   side meat

1 teaspoon salt
1 can (14½ ounces) tomatoes,
   drained and chopped
1 tablespoon molasses

Wash the beans and place them in a pot with the water and side meat. Place over medium heat and let come to a boil, then reduce to low heat and cook for 2 hours, until tender, adding water as needed to keep the beans moist. Remove the seasoning meat and add the salt, tomatoes, and molasses. Cover and let simmer for 10 minutes.

Serves about 8.

Pickled Beets

2 cans (16 ounces each) sliced
   beets
¼ cup vinegar

½ cup sugar
1 tablespoon pickling spice

Drain the juice from one of the cans of beets into a pot. Add the vinegar, sugar, and pickling spice, stir, and let come to a boil. Remove immediately from the stove. Drain the second can of beets; discard the juice and add the beets from both cans to the pot. Let the beets cool and then refrigerate until ready to serve.

Field Creasy Greens

You can find bunches of these scallop-edged leaves in the field from about December through February. (To avoid unpleasant surprises, take along someone who knows how to identify creasy greens if you aren't sure what you're looking for.) They are cold-weather greens. You cut creasies as if you were cutting a cabbage head, leaving the bunch together. Take out all the dry leaves and dirt. Split the root end and let soak in the sink in warm water. Creasies need a lot of washing—five times. If you buy these greens from a grocer, they usually have long stems, which you will need to cut off. About 3 pounds of field creasies makes 4 to 6 servings; buy 4 pounds if there are long stems to cut off. Leave plenty of juice for pot liquor.

Wash a country ham hock, put it in a pot with water to cover, and let come to a boil. Turn the heat down and simmer for about 1 hour or until the hock is tender. Add greens to the pot, along with 4 cups water. Stir. Let come to a boil, cover, and turn the heat to low. Let the greens cook for 45 minutes. Remove the hock from the pot and slice the lean part of the ham and serve with the greens. Serve the pot liquor on the side for dunking cornbread.

Country Spring Green Cabbage Vegetable Pot

For country fresh, buy cabbage at a farmers' market in springtime. Serve this with dog bread patties and the pot liquor.

2 tablespoons oil
1 cup finely sliced lean ham pieces
1 quart water
1 green cabbage (2 pounds)

1 pound small new potatoes, peeled or scraped
3 carrots, cut into pieces

Wash the ham and place it in a pot with the oil. Cook slowly over medium low heat until brown. Add the water and bring to a boil. Reduce the heat to very low and simmer for 20 minutes. Remove the ham and set it aside. Tear away the few outer leaves of the cabbage and cut the head into 8 pieces. Put the cabbage into the pot, along with the potatoes and carrots, and cover. Let cook slowly for 20 to 25 minutes, turning the vegetables lightly to cook evenly. If you wish, you can add the ham pieces back to the pot and heat before serving.

Serves 6 to 8.

Quick Cabbage—Country Style

2 strips lean country side meat
2 tablespoons oil
1 cabbage (2 pounds)

¼ cup water
salt to taste

Wash and shred the cabbage and place it in cold water until ready to use. Put the side meat in a pot with the oil and cook slowly until crispy. Drain the cabbage and add it to the pot along with the ¼ cup water. Cook on low for 15 minutes, stirring to cook evenly. Add salt to taste.

Serves 6.

Nine-Day Sauerkraut

*On the farm, when cabbages were plentiful, we would fill a big stone
or wooden keg with shredded cabbage, salt, and water. The green outer
leaves of the cabbages were spread on top. Then we covered the keg, with
the top weighed down with a rock, to let the kraut ripen. Later we put it
in jars for the winter.*

Fill and pack as many quart jars as you like with shredded cabbage.
For each jar, add 1 teaspoon salt and fill with boiling water, filling only to
the shoulder of the jar. Seal the jars and let sit for at least 9 days. When
you are ready to use the sauerkraut, drain it and simmer it with 2 tablespoons drippings from bacon or salt pork and 2 cups water for 30 to
35 minutes. Or boil it with fresh pork neck bones. Boil neck bones for
30 minutes, skim the fat off, add 1 red pepper and the sauerkraut, and
let cook 20 minutes more on low.

Cauliflower

Pick cauliflower that is white and free of brown spots.

1 large head of cauliflower	1 teaspoon garlic salt
1 teaspoon dried dill	½ stick butter, melted

Remove the leaves from the cauliflower and cut it into florets. Put the
florets in a bowl with cold salt water. Let sit for 10 to 15 minutes, then
rinse. Put the florets in a pot and cover with hot water. Cook over
medium heat, covered, for 10 minutes or until just tender. Drain. Stir
the dill and garlic salt into the melted butter and pour over the cauliflower. Mix lightly.

Serves 4 to 6.

Collard Greens

We didn't grow collard greens on our farm in Chatham County. Collards came to this area after World War II, maybe in the 1950s. This is a cold-weather vegetable — the flavor is best after October.

3 pounds collard greens	1 quart hot water
1 cup lean ham pieces	2 teaspoons salt
3 tablespoons vegetable oil	1 teaspoon sugar (optional)

Wash the collard greens, remove the stems and any bad spots, and then chop or shred. Cook the ham pieces slowly in the oil until crisp. Add the water and simmer for about 10 minutes. Remove the ham and set it aside. Add the salt, sugar, and collard greens to the pot. Turn the heat to medium high and let the water begin to boil. Stir, then turn the heat to low. Let the greens cook slowly, adding a little hot water if needed to keep them moist, until tender, about 45 minutes. Mash a stem to check for tenderness. Once the collards are tender, you can chop them smaller before serving if you like. You can also add the ham to the greens if you wish.

Serves 6 to 8.

Fried Okra

1 pound fresh okra

1 cup self-rising cornmeal

½ cup self-rising flour

1 cup vegetable oil

Rinse the okra and dry with a paper towel. Cut the pods into ½-inch pieces, removing the tops. In a bowl, mix together the cornmeal, flour, and salt. Add the okra pieces to the bowl, stirring to coat with the cornmeal mixture, and then let sit for a few minutes. Stir again. When the breading clings to the okra, shake the bowl—the excess breading will go to the bottom. Heat the oil over medium high heat in a frying pan large enough to allow the okra room to cook evenly. Spoon the okra out of the bowl and fry in the hot oil until browned all over, about 10 to 15 minutes. Drain the okra on paper towels before serving.

Serves 6.

Buttered Okra

1 pound fresh okra

1 cup water

½ stick butter or margarine, cut into pieces

1 teaspoon salt

In a pot, add the butter and salt to the water and bring to a boil over medium heat. Add the okra. Cover the pot and let the okra simmer for 8 to 10 minutes or just until tender. Stir occasionally to cook evenly. Serve in the cooking liquid.

Serves 4 to 6.

Country-Style Brussels Sprouts with Whole Baby Okra

Brussels sprouts are a cool-weather vegetable, best from October to March. The outside leaves should be green and not withered, except for the outermost leaves that you would cut off anyway. When preparing fresh sprouts, cut off a little of the stem end and soak the sprouts for 15 minutes in 1 quart cold water with 2 teaspoons salt. Cut the sprouts in half and rinse in plain water. If using frozen brussels sprouts, let them thaw, cut off the stem, and split in half. Use fresh or frozen okra.

¼ cup lean country ham (look for scrap pieces at the meat counter in the grocery), cut into thin strips

2 tablespoons vegetable oil

2 cups water

salt to taste

1 teaspoon sugar

¼ teaspoon crushed red pepper (optional)

1½–2 pounds fresh brussels sprouts or 3 packages (10 ounces each) frozen brussels sprouts

8–10 pods fresh or frozen baby okra, stem end removed

Use a pot that is 10 to 12 inches wide at the bottom (country pots were big at the bottom). Wash the ham pieces and put them into the pot with the oil over low heat. Spread out the ham pieces to cook evenly. Let the ham cook until crisp, stirring as it cooks. Add the water, salt, sugar, and, if you like, red pepper. Turn the heat to medium high and let the water come to a boil. Put in the brussels sprouts and cook, stirring now and then, until all the ingredients are hot, about 10 minutes. Place the okra on top of the brussels sprouts and cover the pot. Cook slowly for another 10 to 15 minutes.

Serves about 6 to 8.

Note: True to its country origins, this dish can be varied according to the vegetables you like or have on hand. Try making it with new potatoes or baby squash added to the pot; or make it with the brussels sprouts alone.

Okra and Tomatoes

This vegetable dish is on the menu daily at Mama Dip's Kitchen. If fresh vegetables aren't available, you can substitute a 10-ounce package of frozen okra and a 14½-ounce can of tomatoes.

2 cups ½-inch pieces of fresh okra
½ cup water
3 cups diced fresh tomatoes

½ stick butter or margarine, cut into pieces
salt to taste

Place the okra in a pot with the water and let come to a boil. Add the tomatoes, butter, and salt to the okra, stirring to mix well. Simmer for 12 to 15 minutes.

If you use canned tomatoes, cut them up before adding to the pot and add the juice along with the tomatoes. Add the okra and the butter but not the salt (canned tomatoes have enough salt). Cook over medium heat for 10 to 12 minutes.

Serves 4 to 6.

Country Bonnet Green Peas with Dumplings

Garden peas were one of the first vegetables, along with spring onions and asparagus, to come up in early spring. Garden peas cooked with dumplings were a real treat that I remember fondly. For old-fashioned country taste, you need fresh shelled peas and butter.

3 cups fresh shelled green peas (about 3 pounds) or 2 packages (10 ounces each) frozen green peas
1 quart water
1 teaspoon salt
½ stick butter, cut into pieces

DUMPLINGS:
1 cup all-purpose flour
⅓ cup warm broth from cooking peas

Put the peas in a pot with the water, salt, and butter. Cook slowly until the peas are tender, about 25 minutes. For the dumplings, take ⅓ cup broth from the peas and, using a fork or your fingertips, combine with the flour to form a dough. Roll the dough out very thin (not more than ⅛ inch thick) and cut into strips. Then cut the strips into 1-inch pieces and drop them into the pot along with the boiling peas. Shake the pot. Add a little hot water if needed, cover, and turn heat to simmer for another 10 minutes.

Serves about 6.

Dried Black-Eyed Peas

Black-eyed peas are an important part of the traditional New Year's meal, served alongside hog jowl and collard greens. I've always heard the explanation of the meal, passed down from generation to generation through the grapevine, given this way: the black-eyed peas symbolize change or silver coins, the collard greens are greenbacks or paper money, and the hog jowl wards off bad luck. This meal is served at Mama Dip's Kitchen every New Year. I have never had the nerve to ask anyone, "Do you believe, or is it just good eating?"

1 pound dried black-eyed peas
4 ounces salt pork
2 quarts water

1 tablespoon finely chopped onion
1 teaspoon salt
½ teaspoon crushed red pepper

Soak the black-eyed peas in warm water for 2 hours. While the peas are soaking, put the salt pork into a pot with the water and let come to a boil. Reduce the heat to low and let simmer for 45 minutes. Add the peas, onion, salt, and, if you like, crushed red pepper. Let cook for about 45 minutes, adding water if needed.

Serves 6 to 8.

Hoppin' John

I like making this dish with fresh shelled or frozen black-eyed peas because it doesn't get as dry that way as it does if you use dried peas.

1 pound fresh pork neck bones
4 cups fresh black-eyed peas or
   3 packages (10 ounces each)
   frozen black-eyed peas
1 cup finely chopped onion

1 teaspoon garlic salt
½ teaspoon dried thyme
½ teaspoon crushed red pepper
1 cup rice, uncooked

Wash the neck bones, put in a pot with enough water to cover them, and let come to a boil. Turn the heat to low and cook slowly until tender, about 1 hour. Remove the neck bones from the pot, skim off the fat, and strain the liquid. If necessary, add water to the broth to make 4 cups liquid. Put the liquid back into the pot and add the peas, onion, garlic salt, thyme, and red pepper. Let come to a boil. Put in the rice. Stir well and cover. Reduce the heat to low and let cook slowly for about 30 minutes. Meanwhile, pick the meat off the neck bones. Add it to the peas and rice for a one-dish meal.

Serves 8.

Rice Casserole

1 small box wild rice
½ cup white rice
½ cup finely chopped celery
¼ cup finely chopped onion

2 tablespoons butter or margarine
½ cup sliced fresh mushrooms
1½ cups grated cheddar cheese

Cook both kinds of rice according to package directions. While the rice is cooking, sauté the celery and onions together in the butter until tender, about 10 minutes. Do not brown. Add the mushrooms and cook for 1 minute more. Combine the vegetables and both kinds of rice, stirring well to mix. Place half of the rice mixture in the bottom of a casserole dish. Spread half of the cheese over the rice. Put in the remaining rice mixture and cover with the remaining cheese. Bake in a 350° oven long enough to melt the cheese, about 15 minutes.

Serves 6 to 8.

Brown Rice with Vegetables

1¼ cups brown rice
¾ stick butter
1½ cups finely chopped celery
1 cup chopped onion

1 can (10¾ ounces) beef broth
½ teaspoon Kitchen Bouquet
  browning and gravy sauce

Cook the rice according to package directions. Place the butter, celery, and onion in a saucepan. Cook over medium heat until the vegetables are tender. Mix water with the broth and Kitchen Bouquet. Mix all the ingredients together. Heat on low until warmed through.

Serves 4 to 6.

Poke Salad and Spring Onions

Poke salad used to pop up at Easter time around the barn or in other dry, rich places on the farm. Pokeweed grows fast—when 12 inches tall, it is still tender and good to cook. When it grows taller than that, it should not be harvested and eaten. It really shrinks when you cook it, so you need 6 to 8 bunches to make 4 servings. When the poke plant gets full-grown, it has bunches of purple berries. We never ate the berries and were told they are poisonous. They were used to dye flour sacks for quilt linings.

6–8 bunches poke salad	2 bunches spring onions
1 tablespoon salt	3 tablespoons bacon fat

Pull the poke leaves off the stems and wash them. Put them in a large pot, half filled with hot water. Bring to a boil and let boil for 10 minutes. Drain and rinse well. Fill the pot half full with hot water once again. Add the salt and poke leaves. Let sit for 15 minutes; meanwhile, prepare the onions. Slice the spring onions, including the green tops. Sauté the onions in the bacon fat until just tender. Drain the water from the pot containing the poke salad and add the onions, with the bacon fat in which they've been cooked. Mix well. Let simmer 10 to 12 minutes.

Serves 4.

Fresh Turnip Greens

Buy greens that are not withered. Fresh turnip greens should have good green color with green stems. If the stems are purple and the leaves are little, the greens didn't grow fast enough and will usually be tough.

2½ pounds fresh turnip greens	4 cups hot water
2 slices salt pork (¼ inch thick and 3 inches long)	salt to taste

To get the greens ready for cooking, first pick out the large stems. Rinse the leaves in cold water containing 1 tablespoon salt. Repeat 3 or 4 times, then drain the greens. Place the greens in a large pot with 4 cups hot water, pushing them down at the sides (the hot water will make them shrink faster). Let cook over medium heat until tender, about 45 minutes. But occasionally check the stems for tenderness after about 20 minutes, as some greens harvested in the spring of the year take only that long to cook. Remove the greens from the pot and chop them, using a sharp knife and a fork. In another pot, fry the salt pork until done on both sides. Remove the salt pork, leaving the drippings. Place the greens in the drippings and add the salt. Simmer for 15 minutes, adding 2 or 3 tablespoons hot water if needed.

Serves 4 to 6.

Fresh Turnip Greens with Turnips

3 pounds fresh turnip greens
3 slices salt pork (3 inches long and ¼ inch thick)
1½ pounds turnips, peeled and diced
salt to taste
4 cups water

Fill a large pot halfway with hot water. Wash, cook, and chop the greens as in the preceding recipe. Set the greens aside. In a skillet or 2-quart pot, cook the salt pork until done on both sides. Remove the salt pork, leaving the drippings. Place the greens in the pot with the salt pork drippings, put in the diced turnips, and add the water and salt. Cover, reduce the heat to low, and let cook until the turnips are just tender, about 30 minutes.

Serves 6 to 8.

Spinach

2½ pounds fresh spinach
1 cup hot water

1 teaspoon garlic salt
½ stick butter, cut into pieces

Pick over the spinach to remove any weeds and brown leaves. Break off large stems (small, tender stems can remain). Place the spinach leaves in a sink filled with cold water. Let sit for 10 minutes to loosen grit. Wash three times, changing the water each time, until all grit is gone. Place the spinach in a pot with the water and garlic salt. Let come to a boil. Cook for 10 to 15 minutes, stirring to cook evenly. Drain and add the butter, stirring lightly to mix.

Serves 4.

Spinach Casserole

4 packages (10 ounces each)
  frozen chopped spinach,
  thawed
1 can (10¾ ounces) condensed
  cream of mushroom soup

1 teaspoon garlic salt
½ cup milk
2 eggs, beaten
¼ stick butter, melted
3 tablespoons Parmesan cheese

Preheat oven to 350°. Mix all the ingredients together well and pour into a 2-quart baking dish. Bake for 45 minutes.

Serves 6 to 8.

Broccoli Casserole

3 packages (10 ounces each)
 frozen chopped broccoli,
 thawed
1 can (10¾ ounces) condensed
 cream of mushroom soup
¼ cup mayonnaise

2 eggs, beaten
1 teaspoon garlic salt
1 cup grated cheddar cheese
1 cup cracker crumbs, mixed
 evenly with 2 tablespoons
 melted butter or margarine

Preheat oven to 350°. Mix together all the ingredients except the cracker crumbs, combining them well. Put into a 2-quart casserole dish. Sprinkle the buttered crumbs over the top. Bake for 35 minutes.

Serves 6 to 8.

Tomato Casserole

In the country, we served this as a vegetable, but it's made like a dessert. Nowadays it's called stewed tomatoes. It's great with pork.

6 cups fresh tomatoes, peeled and
 diced, or 2 cans (14½ ounces
 each) tomatoes, drained
1½ cups bread cubes

¼ teaspoon black pepper
½ stick butter, melted
¼ cup brown sugar

Mix all the ingredients together lightly in a baking dish. Bake uncovered in a 400° oven for 30 to 40 minutes.

Serves 6.

Note: Tomatoes are a hardy bearing vegetable that can be used frozen.

Zucchini Casserole

1½ pounds zucchini, washed and
    sliced
¼ cup chopped onion
½ stick butter, cut into pieces

3 eggs, beaten well
1 cup milk
½ cup grated Parmesan cheese

Put the squash and onion in a pot with very little water. Cover and cook, stirring often, until tender. Drain, add the butter, and mash with a fork or potato masher. Add the milk and Parmesan cheese. Mix well. Slowly stir in the beaten eggs. Pour into a 1½-quart baking dish and bake in a 350° oven on the lower rack for 40 minutes.

Serves 6.

Squash Casserole

Use either zucchini or yellow squash. Frozen squash may be used instead of fresh.

2 pounds squash, washed and
    sliced, or 2 family packs
    (1 pound each) frozen squash
¼ cup finely chopped onion
1 can (10½ ounces) chicken broth

3 tablespoons cornstarch
½ stick butter, cut into pieces
1 cup bread crumbs, mixed evenly
    with 2 tablespoons melted
    butter or margarine

Cook the squash with the onion as in the preceding recipe. Drain. Heat the chicken broth in a small pot. Mix the cornstarch with a little water (enough to make a paste) and stir into the hot broth. Add the butter and cook until thickened. Combine the thickened sauce with the squash and pour into a 9 × 13-inch casserole dish.

Sprinkle the buttered bread crumbs on top. Bake in a 350° oven on the lower rack for 40 minutes, until brown on top.

Serves 6 to 8.

Summer Squash with Onions

Use either yellow crooked-neck squash or zucchini. When buying squash, be sure they are not too large or too dark in color. Squash needs little or no water when cooked covered.

2 pounds yellow squash or zucchini
½ stick butter or margarine, cut into pieces,
   or 3 tablespoons bacon drippings
1 cup chopped onion
salt to taste

Wash the squash under cold running water while rubbing your hands over the squash to remove any grit. Cut the squash into ½-inch slices and place in a pan or bowl of cold water. Dip the squash slices out of the water and put them in a pot with the butter, onion, and salt. Cover and cook over medium heat for 15 minutes, stirring often. Turn off the heat and let the flavor ripen for 15 minutes.

Serves 6 to 8.

Dill Baby Squash

Pick small baby yellow squash, 2½ to 3 inches long.

1½ pounds baby squash

½ stick margarine, cut into pieces

2 tablespoons water

1 teaspoon dried dill

salt to taste

Wash the squash under running water, rubbing your hands over the squash to remove any grit. Cut off the tip on both ends and split each squash in half lengthwise. Put into a 2-quart pot with the margarine, water, dill, and salt. Cover and let cook over medium heat for 12 to 15 minutes, stirring occasionally.

Serves 6.

Fried Squash

Use sliced yellow squash or zucchini.

1 pound squash, washed and
   sliced

1 teaspoon salt

1 egg, beaten

1 cup milk

2 cups cornmeal

¼ cup self-rising flour

1 teaspoon dried celery leaves,
   crushed

vegetable oil for frying

Sprinkle the squash slices with the salt. Mix the egg and milk together in a bowl. Put in the squash and stir lightly to coat. Mix together the cornmeal, flour, and celery leaves. Batter the squash slices by dipping them in the cornmeal mixture. Heat oil, 1 inch deep, in a frying pan over medium high heat; add the squash slices in increments and fry. Remove slices as they brown and add more until all are cooked. Do not crowd the squash in the pan, so that they can cook evenly.

Serves 6.

Stuffed Squash

Use zucchini that are about 4 to 5 inches long and 2 inches wide.

4 zucchini
½ cup cracker or bread crumbs, mixed evenly with 1 tablespoon melted butter or margarine

STUFFING:
¼ stick butter
1 tablespoon cornstarch or flour
¼ cup sour cream
½ teaspoon dried dill
salt to taste
squash pulp

Cook the squash whole for 15 minutes in boiling water with 2 teaspoons salt. Pour off the hot water and cover the squash with cold water to stop them from cooking. When the squash are cool, cut them in half lengthwise, scoop out the insides (reserving them in a bowl), and drain the hollow shells on paper towels. Mash the insides with a fork. To make the stuffing, melt the butter in a saucepan. Stir in the cornstarch, then stir in the sour cream, dill, and salt. Mix in the squash pulp and then spoon the mixture evenly into the zucchini shells. Sprinkle the buttered crumbs on top. Bake in a 350° oven for 30 minutes.

Serves 6 to 8.

Potatoes with Spring Onions

Serve with fish or barbecue.

2 pounds potatoes, peeled and
    sliced
2 teaspoons salt
¾ stick butter, cut into pieces

1 cup sliced spring onion
    (including tender green tops)
black pepper to taste

Cook the potatoes in water with the salt, using just enough water to cover the potatoes. Boil for 15 minutes. Add the butter, put in the onions and pepper, and stir to mix well. Cover and reduce the heat to simmer for 10 minutes.

Serves 6.

Mashed Potatoes

Mashed potatoes with gravy is as southern as apple pie!

2 pounds white potatoes
¾ stick butter or margarine,
    cut into pieces

¾ cup milk (maybe less)
salt to taste

Wash and peel the potatoes, then cut into quarters. Put the potatoes into a pot, cover with water, and boil until tender, about 20 minutes. Drain. Add the butter and mash the potatoes well, using a potato masher. With a wire whisk or electric mixer, add the milk, a little at a time, until the potatoes are as soft as you like.

Serves 6 to 8.

Mayonnaise New Potatoes

When mayonnaise first came to our country store in Chatham County, we used it on small, newly dug potatoes when the butter was low. Very tasty!

2 pounds white new potatoes, scraped or peeled
4 tablespoons mayonnaise
1 teaspoon salt plus salt to taste

Boil the potatoes (leave them whole) in water with 1 teaspoon salt until tender, about 25 minutes. Drain. Mix together the mayonnaise and salt to taste and stir into the potatoes.

Serves 6.

Creamed New Potatoes

You will find these small new potatoes in grocery stores from about February to July. Use either red-skinned or white potatoes.

2 pounds new potatoes, peeled or scraped
1 teaspoon salt
½ cup milk
½ stick butter, cut into pieces
2 teaspoons flour or cornstarch, mixed with a little water to make a paste
½ teaspoon black pepper

Put the potatoes in a pot with water and the salt and boil until tender, about 15 minutes. Drain off all the water. Add the milk and butter. Let come to a boil over medium heat. Slowly add the flour paste, a bit at a time, and stir, using only as much paste as necessary to make the cooking liquid creamy. Sprinkle with the black pepper. Cover and let simmer for 5 minutes.

Serves 6.

Home-Fried Potatoes with Onions

Just right at breakfast time.

2 pounds white potatoes, washed,
   peeled, and chopped
1 teaspoon salt
1 large onion, chopped

1 green pepper, chopped
   (optional)
bacon fat or margarine for frying

Place the potatoes in a pot with water and the salt. Bring to a boil over medium heat and cook until tender, about 15 minutes. Drain. Heat the bacon fat or margarine in a skillet or frying pan. Add the potatoes, onion, and, if you like, green pepper. Let cook slowly to brown. Using a spatula, divide the potatoes into servings and turn them over to brown the other side.

Serves 6 to 8.

Old-Fashioned Candied Yams

Although yams and sweet potatoes are actually two different vegetables, most people, especially in the South, use the names interchangeably, and sweet potatoes have traditionally been used in the dish known as candied yams — and in all dishes with "yam" or "sweet potato" in their name. For candied yams, they were cooked in cast-iron pans, and when they were done, they would be brown, thick, crispy, and sticky. Here they are made in a baking dish in the oven.

1½ pounds sweet potatoes,
   peeled and thinly sliced
¼ cup sugar

½ stick butter, melted
¼ cup water

Wash the potatoes. Peel and thinly slice them one at a time, placing the slices in a bowl or pan of cold water to keep their color. Put the raw potato slices in a 9 × 13-inch baking dish. Mix together the other ingredients and spoon them over the potatoes. Put in a 375° oven on the lower rack and let cook, uncovered, for 35 to 40 minutes. The yams should have little or no juice when done.

Serves 4 to 6.

Stove-Top Yams

If you are in a hurry, this is a time-saver.

2 pounds fresh sweet potatoes	1 tablespoon self-rising flour
1 cup sugar	¾ cup water
1 teaspoon nutmeg	½ stick butter, cut into pieces

Wash the potatoes. Peel and slice them one at a time, placing the slices in a bowl or pan of cold water to keep their color. In a bowl, mix together the sugar, nutmeg, and flour. Drain the potato slices and put them in a pot. Sprinkle the sugar mixture over them. Add the water and butter. Let the potatoes come to a boil, reduce the heat, cover, and let simmer until tender, about 20 minutes. Stir lightly and serve.

Serves 6.

Sweet Potato Casserole

3 pounds sweet potatoes, cooked
  and mashed
1 cup sugar
¾ stick butter, melted
½ cup milk
2 eggs, beaten
1 package lemon-flavored
  Kool-Aid mix

TOPPING:
1 cup brown sugar
1 cup chopped pecans
1 tablespoon cinnamon

Combine all the ingredients except those for the topping; mix well. Put into a 9 × 13-inch casserole dish. Mix the topping ingredients and sprinkle evenly over the potatoes. Bake in a 375° oven for 30 to 40 minutes.

Serves 8 to 10.

Cheese Sauce

Serve over almost any vegetable.

1 cup milk
1 tablespoon cornstarch
2 tablespoons water
½ stick butter or margarine, cut
  into pieces

1 cup (4 ounces) shredded
  cheddar cheese
1 tablespoon Parmesan cheese
1 teaspoon salt

Put the milk in a saucepan over medium high heat. Combine the cornstarch and water, blending until smooth. When the milk gets hot, stir in the cornstarch mixture. Turn the heat to low and add the butter, both cheeses, and the salt. Cook until the cheese is melted and the sauce is heated through.

Makes 1¼ cups.

Salads and Salad Dressings

The salads included here are essential hot-weather side dishes. Many of the recipes include traditional salad ingredients—lettuce, tomatoes, cucumbers—but the full gamut of vegetables is represented. Because they are served cold, these salads are ideal vegetable dishes for picnics, potluck dinners, or family reunions.

Potato Salad

Potato salad is best made with new potatoes. It can be made year round, but make sure your potatoes are not sprouting. Use potatoes that are all about the same size so they will cook evenly.

2½ pounds new potatoes,
  washed but unpeeled
1 teaspoon salt
1 teaspoon celery seed or ½ cup
  chopped celery
3 hard-boiled eggs, grated
1 cup sweet pickle relish

1 medium jar (4 ounces) pimento,
  chopped
½ cup mayonnaise
2 teaspoons prepared mustard
¼ cup chopped spring onion
  (optional)

Put the potatoes in a pot with enough water to cover them and cook until tender, about 35 minutes or less, according to size. Drain off the hot water and pour in cold water to cool the potatoes. When they are cool enough to handle, peel and dice the potatoes and place them in a large bowl. Add all the other ingredients and mix well. Refrigerate until ready to serve.

Serves about 10.

Spring Garden Potato Salad

Good for brunch or a church supper. It's best to use small new potatoes for this recipe.

2 pounds red new potatoes, leaving on some peel
2 teaspoons salt
1 cup thinly sliced spring onion (including tender green tops)
½ cup mayonnaise

Wash the potatoes. Peel them partially, put them in a pot, and cover with hot water. Add the salt. Let come to a boil and turn heat to medium to cook slowly for 20 minutes—check for doneness according to the size of the potatoes. Drain. Put some ice cubes in the pot to help cool the potatoes and let sit for 10 minutes. Drain well. Put the potatoes into a bowl and stir in the mayonnaise. Lightly stir in the onions. Serve warm or refrigerate until ready to serve.

Serves 8.

Vegetable Salad

2 cups broccoli florets
3 small zucchini
3 medium yellow squash
1 small cauliflower
4 small carrots
2 medium cucumbers

DRESSING:
¼ cup wine vinegar
¼ cup vegetable oil
1 teaspoon black pepper
1 tablespoon dry mustard
salt to taste

Wash and dry all the vegetables and dice into small pieces. Place them in a large bowl. In a small bowl, combine the dressing ingredients, using a wire whisk to mix them well. Pour the dressing over the diced vegetables and toss to coat. Serve immediately or refrigerate until ready to serve.

Serves about 8 to 10.

Cucumbers, Tomatoes, and Onions

You would see this at every meal all through the summer at our house. Set this on the table when serving fresh, cooked vegetables.

2 medium onions
2 cucumbers
3 fresh tomatoes

1 teaspoon salt
black pepper to taste
¼ cup vinegar

Slice the onions and cucumbers, and dice the tomatoes. Mix together in a bowl. Add the salt, pepper, and vinegar. Toss to marinate. Refrigerate until ready to serve.

Serves about 6 to 8.

Luncheon Salad

1 pound red delicious apples, cored and diced
½ cup thinly sliced celery
½ cup raisins, rinsed in warm water and dried with a paper towel
2 spring onions, thinly sliced (do not include green tops)
½ pound luncheon meat (turkey, chicken, or ham)

DRESSING:
¼ cup mayonnaise
¼ cup plain yogurt

Dice the apples and place them in a bowl; add the celery, raisins, and onion. Cut the meat into strips and add to the bowl. Mix the dressing ingredients together, spoon over the other ingredients, and toss, mixing well. Chill and serve on lettuce.

Serves 6 to 8.

Broccoli and Cauliflower Salad

This salad is served daily at Mama Dip's Kitchen.

3 cups broccoli florets
3 cups cauliflower florets
½ red onion, sliced

DRESSING:

1 cup mayonnaise or salad
    dressing (such as Miracle Whip)
3 tablespoons vinegar
3 tablespoons powdered sugar
pinch salt

Wash the vegetables in cold water. Drain them, then put them in cold water to soak for 15 minutes. Drain and refrigerate until ready to dress and serve. When ready to serve, mix all of the dressing ingredients together well, pour over the vegetables, and stir lightly to coat.

Serves about 6 to 8.

Pistachio Salad

A pretty salad to serve at Christmas time.

2 boxes (3.4 ounces each) Jell-O pistachio instant pudding mix
1 can (15 ounces) crushed pineapple, with juice
2 containers (8 ounces each) whipped topping
1 cup chopped pecans
1 cup miniature marshmallows

In a large bowl, stir the dry pudding mix together with the pineapple. Fold in the whipped topping, pecans, and marshmallows. Refrigerate at least 1 hour or until ready to serve.

Serves 6 to 8.

October Bean and Tomato Salad

You will find October beans at farmers' markets from about August through October. They look like green pinto beans.

1 pound October beans
1 can (10¾ ounces) chicken broth
4 large, firm fresh tomatoes, diced
1 bunch spring onions, sliced
   (not including the green tops)
1 red bell pepper, seeded and
   sliced thin

2 cloves garlic, finely chopped
3 tablespoons chopped fresh
   parsley
1 tablespoon sugar
¼ cup vinegar
½ cup vegetable oil
1 teaspoon black pepper

Wash the beans and cook them in chicken broth, adding hot water as necessary to cover the beans, for about 40 minutes or until tender. Let the beans cool, then combine them with all the other ingredients in a large bowl, mixing well. Let ripen in the refrigerator for 1 hour before serving.

Serves about 6 to 8.

Tossed Green Salad Bowl

1 head Romaine lettuce, washed
   and torn into pieces
½ pound spinach, washed and
   torn into pieces
1 cup sliced celery

½ carrot, thinly sliced
1 cup shredded red cabbage
1 cucumber, thinly sliced
1 bunch spring onions, thinly
   sliced (without the green tops)

Mix all of the ingredients together and refrigerate until ready to serve. Use the dressing of your choice.

Serves 8.

Cucumber and Spinach Salad

¾ pound spinach, washed and
   torn into pieces
2 large cucumbers, thinly sliced
1 bunch spring onions, sliced
   (including some of the green
   tops)
1 small can (11 ounces) mandarin
   oranges, drained

DRESSING:
½ cup plain yogurt
1 cup sour cream
½ teaspoon salt

Mix together the yogurt, sour cream, and salt and place them in the refrigerator. Reserve some of the spring onion to use as a garnish. Combine the rest of the onion with the spinach, cucumbers, and oranges and refrigerate to crisp. When ready to serve, place individual portions of the salad on plates and spoon the dressing over the salad. Sprinkle a bit of the sliced spring onion on top.

Serves 4 to 6.

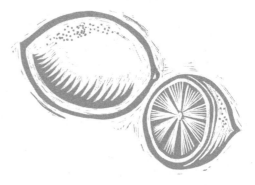

Tomato Jam

Here's something to do with all those tomatoes you've grown. Good with lamb.

6 cups ripe tomatoes
6 cups sugar
1 teaspoon ginger

¼ cup lemon juice
2 teaspoons lemon rind

Pour boiling water over the tomatoes, then dip them into cold water to loosen the peels. Peel and seed the tomatoes and cut them into chunks. Place them in a large pot and add the sugar, ginger, lemon juice, and lemon rind. Cook over medium heat until the sugar dissolves, then turn the heat up and let the tomatoes come to a rolling boil; turn the heat back down and let simmer for 45 minutes, stirring often so the tomatoes will not stick. Store in sterile half-pint jars (approximately 5).

Vinegar Dressing

¼ cup water
½ cup wine vinegar
1 cup vegetable oil

2 teaspoons salt
1 tablespoon dry mustard
1 teaspoon black pepper

Place all of the ingredients in a bowl and mix well using a wire whisk or hand-held mixer. Refrigerate until ready to use.

Blue Cheese Dressing

1 cup mayonnaise

1 cup buttermilk

4 ounces crumbled blue cheese

½ teaspoon garlic salt

Stir the blue cheese into the mayonnaise, mixing well. Stir in the buttermilk and garlic salt. Pour the mixture into a blender and process on medium speed until creamy. Refrigerate until ready to use.

French Dressing

1 cup vegetable oil

½ cup vinegar

½ teaspoon granulated onion

½ teaspoon garlic salt

1 cup ketchup

½ cup brown sugar

Mix all the ingredients together well, using a wire whisk or hand-held mixer, and refrigerate until ready to use.

Thousand Island Dressing

For lunch, try this over head lettuce with a grated hard-boiled egg.

1 cup salad dressing
  (such as Miracle Whip)

1 cup ketchup

½ cup sweet pickle relish

1 small jar (2 ounces) pimentos

½ teaspoon chili powder

Mix all the ingredients together, combining them well. Refrigerate until ready to use.

Desserts,
Beverages, and
Party Dishes

Desserts

I suspect that most people who buy cookbooks go straight to the desserts — they will probably try out a cake recipe even if they never make anything else! At family reunions it sometimes seems that half the buffet table is filled with cakes, pies, and cobblers. Unable to finish off all the goodies at one time, everyone cheerfully wraps up a selection of the leftovers to take home. Nothing is as memorable, or enhances a cook's reputation as much, as a spectacular cake. At my family gatherings, Norma's punch bowl cake takes center stage because it is as pretty as it is yummy and there's always enough to go around.

Cakes and Frostings

Mama Dip's Cake Flour

2 cups self-rising flour
1 cup plain flour
1 teaspoon cornstarch

Sift the ingredients together. Measure before and after sifting.

Basic Three-Layer Cake

2 sticks butter, softened
1 tablespoon shortening
2 cups sugar
4 eggs
3 cups all-purpose flour

1 teaspoon salt
¼ teaspoon baking soda
2 teaspoons baking powder
1 cup milk
1 tablespoon vanilla extract

Preheat oven to 350°. Beat together the butter, shortening, and sugar until very light and creamy. Add the eggs, one at a time, beating well after each addition. Sift the flour, then measure and sift again with the salt, baking soda, and baking powder. Add the dry ingredients alternately with the milk, a little at a time, mixing gently just until well blended. Stir in the vanilla. Pour the batter into three greased and floured 9-inch layer pans and bake for 25 minutes or until a toothpick inserted in the middle of the cake comes out clean. Let cool, then assemble the layers with your favorite frosting.

Serves 12.

Sweet Potato Cake

2 cups self-rising flour
¼ teaspoon baking soda
1 teaspoon cinnamon
1 teaspoon allspice
2 sticks butter, softened
2 cups brown sugar, packed
3 eggs
1 cup milk
1½ cups cooked, mashed
    sweet potato

1 cup raisins, chopped
1 cup chopped pecans

ICING:
1 large can (12 ounces) evaporated
    milk
3 egg yolks
1 cup sugar
1 cup flake coconut

Preheat oven to 350°. Measure the flour, then sift it together with the baking soda and spices. Set aside. Cream the butter and sugar until light and fluffy. Add the eggs, one at a time, and beat well after each addition. Stir in the milk, add the dry ingredients, and mix just until well blended. Mix in the mashed sweet potato. Stir in the raisins and nuts. Pour into three greased 9-inch round or three greased 8 × 8-inch square pans. Bake for 25 minutes or until a toothpick inserted in the center comes out clean. Cool before putting together with the icing.

To make the icing, mix together the evaporated milk, egg yolks, and sugar. Cook over medium heat until thickened, stirring constantly. Stir in the coconut. Spread between the layers and on top of the cake.

Serves 12.

Buttermilk Pound Cake

At family reunions, everyone brings pound cakes — all different kinds!

2 sticks butter, softened	½ teaspoon baking soda
3 cups sugar	1 teaspoon salt
5 eggs	1 teaspoon vanilla extract
1 cup buttermilk	1 teaspoon lemon extract
3 cups all-purpose flour	

Preheat oven to 350°. Cream the butter and sugar until light and fluffy. Add the eggs, one at a time, beating well after each addition. Add the buttermilk and mix well. Sift the flour, baking soda, and salt together and add them to the wet ingredients, stirring gently until well blended. Stir in the vanilla and lemon extracts. Pour the batter into a lightly greased and floured 10-inch tube pan. Bake for 1 hour or until a toothpick inserted in the center comes out clean.

Serves 12.

Chocolate Pound Cake

¼ cup shortening
2 sticks butter, softened
3 cups sugar
5 eggs
3 cups all-purpose flour

½ cup cocoa
1 teaspoon baking powder
1 cup buttermilk
2 teaspoons vanilla extract

Preheat oven to 350°. Cream the shortening, butter, and sugar together until light and fluffy. Add the eggs, one at a time, beating for 1 minute after each addition. Measure the flour and sift it together with the cocoa and baking powder. Sift again. Mix the buttermilk and vanilla together in a cup. Add to the creamed mixture, alternating with the dry ingredients, in thirds. Mix gently just until well blended. Pour into a greased and floured 10-inch tube pan. Bake for about 1 hour and 10 minutes or until a toothpick inserted in the center comes out clean.

Serves 12.

Cold-Oven Rum Pound Cake

The rum glaze makes this pound cake special.

2 sticks butter or margarine,
    softened
¼ cup shortening
3 cups sugar
5 eggs, beaten
3½ cups all-purpose flour
½ teaspoon salt
1 teaspoon baking powder

1 cup milk
1 teaspoon vanilla extract

RUM GLAZE:
½ stick butter, cut into pieces
2 cups 10x powdered sugar
2 tablespoons water
¼ cup dark rum, or 1 minibottle

Do not preheat oven. Cream the butter and shortening well. Add the sugar, beating until light and fluffy. Beat in the eggs, one at a time, beating for 1 minute after each egg is added. Sift together the flour, salt, and baking powder. Beating slowly, add the dry ingredients, alternating with the milk, in thirds, to the creamed mixture until all is mixed in. Stir in the vanilla extract. Pour into a greased and floured 10-inch tube pan and place in a cold oven. Set the oven to 325° and bake for 1 hour and 20 minutes or until a toothpick inserted in the center comes out clean.

For the rum glaze, place the butter and water in a saucepan and heat until the butter melts. Add the sugar and stir while slowly cooking for 2 minutes. Remove from the heat, add the rum, and spoon over the hot cake while it is still in the pan.

Serves 12.

Cream Cheese Pound Cake

2 sticks margarine, softened
1 stick butter, softened
1 package (8 ounces) cream
    cheese, softened
3 cups sugar

6 eggs
2 teaspoons lemon extract
3¼ cups all-purpose flour
½ teaspoon salt

Preheat oven to 325°. In a mixing bowl, beat together the margarine, butter, cream cheese, and sugar until light and fluffy. Add the eggs, one at a time, beating well after each addition. Add the lemon extract. Sift the flour and salt together, then mix into the wet ingredients. Pour the batter into a greased and floured 10-inch tube pan. Bake for 1 hour and 10 minutes or until a toothpick inserted in the center comes out clean. Let the cake cool in the pan, then turn out onto a plate.

Serves 12.

Six-Flavor Pound Cake

This is the best pound cake recipe of all.

2 sticks margarine, softened

3 cups sugar

5 eggs

1 cup milk

1 teaspoon vanilla extract

¼ teaspoon lemon extract

¼ teaspoon ground cloves

¼ teaspoon cinnamon

¼ teaspoon nutmeg

⅛ teaspoon ginger

3 cups all-purpose flour

½ teaspoon salt

Preheat oven to 350°. In a mixing bowl, cream the margarine and sugar, beating until light and fluffy. Add the eggs, one at a time, beating well after each addition. Stir in the milk and the vanilla and lemon extracts. Sift together the spices, flour, and salt; add them to the wet ingredients, stirring gently just until well combined. Pour the batter into a greased and floured 10-inch tube pan and bake for 1 hour and 10 minutes or until a toothpick inserted in the center comes out clean. Let the cake cool in the pan, then turn out onto a plate.

Serves 12.

Italian Cream Cake

2 cups sugar
1 stick butter or margarine,
    softened
½ cup shortening
2 cups plain flour
1 teaspoon baking soda
1 teaspoon salt
1 cup buttermilk
5 egg yolks
2 teaspoons vanilla extract

1 cup chopped walnuts
1 package (7 ounces) flake coconut

ICING:
1 package (8 ounces) cream
    cheese, softened
½ stick butter, softened
1 box (1 pound) 10x powdered
    sugar
2 teaspoons vanilla extract

Preheat oven to 350°. Cream the shortening and butter. Add the sugar,
beating until light and fluffy. Add the egg yolks and beat well, for about
2 minutes. Sift together the flour, baking soda, and salt. Beat in half the
dry ingredients, then half the buttermilk; repeat, making sure that all
of the ingredients are well blended. Fold in the vanilla, walnuts, and
coconut. Pour into three greased and floured 9-inch cake pans. Bake
25 to 30 minutes or until a toothpick inserted in the center comes out
clean. Let cool before icing.

To make the icing, beat together the butter and cream cheese until
well blended. Gradually beat in the powdered sugar, alternating with
the vanilla. Beat until smooth and creamy. Spread between the layers
and on the top and sides of the cake.

Serves 12.

Fresh Apple Cake

This cake needs to be made ahead of time. It's best after three days, when it has had time to mellow.

2 cups peeled and diced apples
1 cup raisins, chopped
1 cup chopped walnuts
1½ cups vegetable oil
2 cups sugar
3 eggs, beaten
3½ cups self-rising flour
2 teaspoons baking powder
1 teaspoon baking soda

1 teaspoon allspice
1 teaspoon vanilla extract

SAUCE:
½ cup buttermilk
½ stick margarine, cut into pieces
½ cup brown sugar, packed
½ teaspoon allspice

Preheat oven to 325°. Dust the apples, raisins, and walnuts with a little flour and set aside. Combine the oil, sugar, and eggs, blending well. Sift together the flour, allspice, baking powder, and baking soda and add to the wet ingredients, stirring gently just until well combined. Stir in the vanilla. Fold in the apples, raisins, and walnuts. Bake in a greased and floured 10-inch tube pan for 1 hour and 15 minutes.

To make the sauce, combine all of the ingredients in a saucepan. Stirring constantly, heat to boiling and let boil rapidly for 2 minutes. Let the sauce cool and then pour it over the cake while the cake is still hot in the pan. Leave the cake in the pan for 1 hour before removing. Wrap the cake in foil or store it in a cakebox. Do not refrigerate. The flavor will ripen and the cake will be ready to serve in three days.

Serves 12.

Carrot Cake

This is my daughter Julia's cake, and it really stands out.

2¼ cups self-rising flour
1 teaspoon baking soda
2½ teaspoons ground cinnamon
2 cups sugar
1½ cups vegetable oil
4 eggs, well beaten
3 cups grated carrots
1 cup chopped walnuts

ICING:

2 packages (8 ounces each) cream
  cheese, softened
1 stick butter, softened
1 box (1 pound) 10x powdered
  sugar
1 teaspoon vanilla extract
1 cup crushed walnuts

Preheat oven to 350°. Sift together the flour, baking soda, and cinnamon. Set aside. Combine the oil and sugar, beating until smooth. Add the eggs and beat until well mixed. Stir in the flour mixture, add the carrots and walnuts, and mix gently just until well combined. Pour the batter into three greased and floured 9-inch cake pans. Bake for 40 minutes or until a wooden toothpick inserted in the center comes out clean. Cool the layers in the pans for 5 minutes, then remove and let them cool completely on wax paper or a wire rack before icing.

To make the icing, beat the butter and cream cheese together until well combined; beat in the powdered sugar, a little at a time, and the vanilla, mixing until smooth. Spread between the layers, sprinkling nuts on top of the icing as you go, and on the top of the cake, sprinkling more nuts on top.

Serves 12.

Mound Cake

2 sticks butter, softened
2 cups sugar
4 eggs
2 squares unsweetened chocolate, melted
2½ cups plain flour
1 teaspoon baking soda
½ teaspoon salt
1 cup buttermilk
2 teaspoons vanilla extract

FILLING:
1 cup milk
¾ cup sugar

8 ounces (half of a large bag) marshmallows
1 package (6 ounces) frozen grated coconut

ICING:
4 squares unsweetened chocolate
1 stick margarine
1 box (1 pound) 10x powdered sugar
2–4 tablespoons warm milk
1 teaspoon vanilla extract
pinch salt

Preheat oven to 350°. Beat together the butter and sugar until light and fluffy. Add the eggs, one at a time, beating well after each addition. Add the chocolate and mix well. Sift together the flour, baking soda, and salt. Add half the dry ingredients, followed by half the buttermilk; repeat, mixing gently until well blended after each addition. Stir in the vanilla. Pour the batter into three greased and floured 9-inch cake pans. Bake for 25 to 30 minutes or until a toothpick inserted in the center comes out clean. Let cool before putting together with filling and icing.

For the filling, mix all of the ingredients together in a saucepan and let cook over medium heat for about 5 minutes, stirring constantly until they are smooth and well combined. Spread between the layers.

For the icing, melt the chocolate and margarine together in a saucepan over low heat, stirring to combine. Remove from heat. Gradually beat in the powdered sugar, alternating with the vanilla and milk (using as much of the milk as necessary to make the icing creamy and spread-able); mix in the salt. Spread over the top and sides of the cake.

Serves 12.

Quick Pineapple-Coconut Upside-Down Cake

1 small box (3.4 ounces) vanilla
   instant pudding mix
1 box (18¼ ounces) yellow cake
   mix with pudding
½ stick butter or margarine

1 cup brown sugar, packed
1 tablespoon cornstarch
1 can (16 ounces) crushed
   pineapple, drained
1 cup flake coconut

Preheat oven to 350°. Stir the pudding mix into the cake mix, then prepare the cake batter according to package directions and set aside. Put the butter, brown sugar, cornstarch, and pineapple in a 9 × 13-inch baking pan. Stir and place in the oven. When the butter is melted, stir to mix the ingredients together well and spread evenly over the bottom of the pan. Sprinkle the coconut over the pineapple mixture and then pour the cake batter evenly on top. Bake on the lowest rack of the oven for 30 minutes or until a toothpick inserted in the center comes out clean. Cool and turn upside down on a serving dish. Serve with whipped topping.

Serves 10 to 12.

Fruit Cake

What a nice Christmas present to give to family or friends! You can make large cakes or smaller loaves, as you prefer.

1 pound raisins

1 pound currants

1 pound candied cherries

1 pound mixed candied fruit peels

½ pound walnut halves or pieces

2 cups dark rum

1 tablespoon frozen orange juice concentrate, undiluted

1 pound butter, softened

2½ cups brown sugar, packed

12 large eggs, separated

2 tablespoons fresh lemon juice

2 tablespoons lemon extract

3¼ cups all-purpose flour

1 teaspoon salt

1½ teaspoons cinnamon

1½ teaspoons allspice

½ teaspoon ground cloves

RUM GLAZE:

1 cup rum (light or dark)

1 cup dark brown sugar, packed

Put the fresh and candied fruit, walnuts, rum, and orange juice into a plastic or other nonmetallic container. Mix well, cover, and let soak for 5 to 7 days (unrefrigerated), stirring the mixture each day.

Preheat oven to 275° for large cakes or 325° for loaves. Cream the butter and sugar. Beat the egg yolks and add to creamed mixture, beating for 4 minutes to blend well. Beat in the lemon juice and lemon extract. Measure the flour and sift together with the salt and spices. Add to the creamed mixture a little at a time, mixing only until smooth. Beat the egg whites until they are stiff but not dry. Fold into the cake batter with a wooden spoon just until blended. Pour into two 10-inch tube pans and bake at 275° for 3½ hours. If you want to make smaller cakes, put the batter in 5 × 9-inch or 3 × 5-inch loaf pans (about 4 pans). Line the pans with greased brown paper bags or greased parchment paper. Bake about 2½ hours at 325°. Test for doneness by inserting a toothpick or knife in the center of the cakes; if it comes out clean, the cakes are done. Let the cakes cool in the pans.

To make the rum glaze, mix the rum and sugar together in a saucepan over medium heat and let simmer for 2 to 3 minutes. Let the glaze cool, then pour it over the cakes while they are still warm in the pans. When the glaze has cooled and hardened, wrap the cakes in plastic wrap and store in an air-tight container.

Punch Bowl Cake Dessert

This is my daughter Norma's dessert. She says put this in a cooler and take it to a big picnic, church supper, or family reunion.

1 large punch bowl
2 frozen pound cakes
  (10¾ ounces each)
1 large can (20 ounces) crushed
  pineapple, drained
2 kiwi fruit, peeled and sliced
2 cans (11 ounces each) mandarin
  oranges, drained

1 quart fresh strawberries, washed,
  hulled, and sliced
1 package (6 ounces) frozen grated
  coconut
2 containers (12 ounces each)
  whipped topping
mint leaves for garnish

Cut each pound cake into 20 slices. Spread about 2 cups of the whipped topping on the bottom of the punch bowl. Layer the fruit, cake slices, and remaining topping in the bowl, ending with whipped topping and a little fruit on top. Garnish with fresh mint leaves. You can add nuts, fruit cocktail, or slices of fresh ripe peaches to the layers, if you like. This is best if made the night before. It may be spooned out or sliced to serve.

Serves about 20.

Chocolate Frosting #1

1 stick butter or margarine, melted
1 box (1 pound) 10x powdered
   sugar
3 tablespoons milk
6 squares unsweetened chocolate,
   melted
½ teaspoon salt
2 teaspoons vanilla extract

Cream together all of the ingredients, beating until blended. Add a little more milk if needed to achieve a spreading consistency.

Makes enough to frost three 9-inch layers.

Chocolate Frosting #2

1 stick butter or margarine
4 tablespoons cocoa
pinch salt
4–5 teaspoons milk
1 box (1 pound) 10x powdered
   sugar
1 teaspoon vanilla extract

In a small saucepan, mix together the butter, cocoa, salt, and milk and cook over medium heat, stirring, until smooth and hot. Remove from the heat and stir in the sugar and vanilla. Add a little more milk if needed to obtain the proper consistency for spreading.

Makes enough to frost three 9-inch layers.

Twelve-Minute Fluffy White Icing

3 cups sugar
1 cup water
1 teaspoon vinegar
3 egg whites
2 cups fresh or frozen grated
   coconut

In a saucepan, combine the sugar, water, and vinegar. Cook over medium heat about 12 minutes, stirring, until it forms fine, hairlike threads that cling to the spoon. In a bowl, beat the egg whites until they begin to foam. Slowly pour the eggs whites in a steady stream into the sugar mixture, beating on the high speed of an electric mixer until the icing holds a stiff peak. Spread immediately on the cake, sprinkling a third of the coconut over each layer, including the top.

Makes enough to frost three 9-inch layers.

Pineapple-Coconut Icing

This is used along with twelve-minute fluffy white icing (see recipe above).

1 can (16 ounces) crushed pineapple, with juice
1 box (1 pound) 10x powdered sugar
½ stick butter or margarine, melted
pinch salt
4 tablespoons milk
1 package (6 ounces) frozen grated coconut

Put the pineapple and its juice in a saucepan and let simmer over low heat for 10 to 12 minutes. Set aside and cool. Mix together the sugar, melted butter, and salt; add the milk, a tablespoon at a time, using only as much as needed to give a good spreading consistency. For each layer of the cake to be frosted, including the top, spread about a quarter of the fluffy white icing, dip or spread with a third of the pineapple mixture, and sprinkle over a third of the coconut. Spread only fluffy white icing around the sides of the cake.

Makes enough to frost three 9-inch layers.

Pies and Cobblers

Fruits and berries of all sorts were the original sweets for country desserts. Country folks gathered wild blackberries, strawberries, or gooseberries in season, and those who didn't have an orchard often planted a few fruit trees near the farmhouse. Some of the fruit would be dried to be used later for pies, turnovers, and such. I remember how from mid-August until late September the ladies would go from house to house preparing apples from each family's tree, almost like a quilting party. The apple slices would be laid out on tin sheets on the south side of the house, protected from dew and rain, for about ten days. When the apples turned brown and seemed dry, they were put into washed flour sacks and hung from a nail on the back porch to keep. The aroma sure made the porch pleasant—guess where we children gathered to play!

Pie Crust for Double Crust

It's best to make pie crust a day ahead and refrigerate it. Or, to make a one-crust recipe, freeze crusts as single pie shells.

2 cups all-purpose flour
½ teaspoon salt

⅔ cup shortening
4 tablespoons cold water

Mix the flour and salt together in a bowl. Add the shortening and mix it into the flour and salt with a fork or your fingertips until the mixture has the texture of coarse crumbs. Mix in the water, a little at a time. Refrigerate to chill before rolling out the dough.

Cherry Meringue Pie

2 cans (16 ounces each) pitted
    cherries
½ cup sugar
pinch salt
1 teaspoon lemon juice
pinch ginger
¼ stick margarine

4 tablespoons cornstarch
1 baked 9-inch pie shell

MERINGUE:
3 egg whites
3 tablespoons 10x powdered sugar
⅛ teaspoon cream of tartar

Drain the juice from the cherries into a pot and stir in the sugar, salt, lemon juice, ginger, and margarine. Bring to a boil over medium heat. Stir a little water into the cornstarch until well blended, then stir slowly into the cherry juice. Simmer until thickened and the juice is clear. Add a drop of red food color if you like. Stir in the cherries. Put the cherry filling into the shell.

To make the meringue, beat the egg whites with an electric mixer on high speed; gradually beat in the sugar and cream of tartar, beating until the whites form peaks. Spread the meringue on top of the cherries and brown in a 400° oven on the lower rack for 10 to 12 minutes.

Serves 8.

Note: You can also make this as tarts. There will be enough filling and meringue for 12 to 15 tart shells.

Dried-Fruit Meringue Pie

1 package (6 ounces) dried apples
    or peaches (best when bought
    at a farmers' market)
2 cups hot water
½ stick butter or margarine
1 cup sugar
1 baked 9-inch pie shell

MERINGUE:
3 egg whites
3 tablespoons 10x powdered sugar
¼ teaspoon cream of tartar

Preheat oven to 400°. Cook the apples or peaches in a saucepan
with the water over low heat. Stir to cook evenly until tender, about
15 minutes. Add a little hot water, if needed to keep the fruit moist.
Add the butter and sugar. Mix well. Pour into the pie shell. Prepare the
meringue as in the preceding recipe and spread it on top of the fruit.
Bake on the lower rack of the oven until brown, about 10 to 12 minutes.

Serves 8.

Old-Time Fried Apple Turnovers

This works well with peaches substituted for the apples, if you prefer.

1 package (6 ounces) dried apples
2 cups hot water
½ stick butter or margarine

½ cup sugar
1 can (10 count) biscuits
vegetable oil for frying

Prepare the filling by cooking the apples and adding the butter and
sugar as in the preceding recipe. Use the biscuits for the turnover
dough. Remove the biscuits from the can, separate them, and let them
come to room temperature. On a floured board, roll out each biscuit
to 3 inches in diameter. Place 2 tablespoons of the apple filling at one
side of the rolled-out biscuit, fold the dough over at the middle, and

press the edges together with a fork. Grease an iron skillet lightly. Over medium low heat, brown the turnovers slowly on both sides. Add a little oil as needed. Or deep-fry at 350°.

Makes 10.

Note: If you have frozen pie crust on hand, you can defrost it and roll it out in 3-inch circles instead of using biscuits.

Pecan Pie

This is the pie that I made on ABC's Good Morning, America.

1 stick butter or margarine	3 eggs, beaten
1 cup sugar	1 cup chopped pecans
1 cup light Karo syrup	1 unbaked 9-inch pie shell

Preheat oven to 350°. In a saucepan, melt the butter but don't let it brown. Mix in the sugar and Karo syrup and cook, stirring, over medium heat until the sugar dissolves. Allow sugar mixture to cool slightly, then stir in the eggs. Mix well. Stir in the pecans. Pour into the pie shell and bake for 1 hour or until firm when shaken.

Serves 8.

Coconut Custard Pie

¾ cup sugar
2 teaspoons self-rising flour
½ teaspoon nutmeg
¼ stick butter or margarine,
    melted
3 eggs, beaten

1 teaspoon vanilla extract
1 cup milk
1 cup fresh or frozen grated
    coconut
1 unbaked 9-inch pie shell

Preheat oven to 375°. In a bowl, blend together the sugar, flour, and nutmeg. Add the butter, eggs, vanilla, and milk. Mix well. Stir in the coconut. Pour into the pie shell and bake for 30 minutes or until firm.

Serves 8.

Egg Custard Pie

This recipe is very old. My first custard pie was made with guinea eggs.

1 cup sugar
2 teaspoons self-rising flour
1 teaspoon nutmeg
¼ stick butter or margarine,
    melted

1 teaspoon vanilla extract
4 eggs, beaten
1 cup milk
1 unbaked 9-inch pie shell

Preheat oven to 375°. In a bowl, mix together the sugar, flour, and nutmeg. Stir in the butter, vanilla, and eggs, and beat for 10 to 15 strokes. Add the milk and mix well. Pour into the pie shell and bake for 30 minutes or until firm.

Serves 8.

Lemon Pie

1 cup sugar

3 tablespoons cornstarch

1 cup milk

3 egg yolks, beaten

½ stick butter or margarine,
 melted

2 tablespoons lemon juice

1 teaspoon grated lemon rind

2 tablespoons light Karo syrup

1 cup sour cream

1 baked 9-inch pie shell

whipped topping

In a saucepan, mix the sugar and cornstarch together. Add the milk, stir, and let stand for 10 minutes to allow the sugar to dissolve. Add the egg yolks and mix well. Stir in the butter, lemon juice, and lemon rind. Cook over medium heat, stirring constantly to prevent sticking, until well thickened. Remove from the heat and let cool. Stir in the Karo syrup and sour cream. Pour into the baked pie shell and refrigerate for at least 1 hour. Top with whipped topping.

Serves 8.

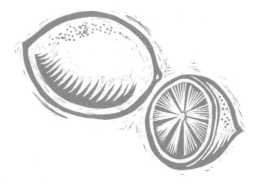

Cheesecake Pies

Top with your favorite pie filling — blueberry and strawberry are good!

3 packages (8 ounces each)
  cream cheese, softened
1 cup sugar
4 eggs, beaten
1 pint sour cream
2 teaspoons vanilla extract
3 prepared 9-inch graham cracker
  crumb crusts

FRUIT TOPPING:
4 tablespoons cornstarch
2 cans (16 ounces each)
  blueberries or 2 packages
  (10 ounces each) frozen
  strawberries

Preheat oven to 325°. Beat together the cream cheese and sugar until light and fluffy. Add the eggs, one at a time, beating well after each egg is added. Add the sour cream, followed by the vanilla. Mix until smooth and creamy. Pour into the crusts and bake for 1 hour.

For the topping, mix the cornstarch and the fruit, along with its juice, in a saucepan. Cook over medium heat until thickened, stirring constantly. Cool and refrigerate until ready to serve over the cheesecake pies.

Each pie serves 5.

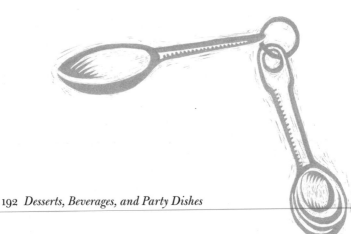

Polka-Dot Pumpkin Pie

I thought that my children wouldn't like pumpkin pie made out of the snaggle-toothed jack-o'-lantern over potato pie, so I added raisins to tempt them—and they liked it.

1 can (15 ounces) pumpkin
2 eggs, well beaten
1 cup brown sugar, packed
1 small can (5 ounces) evaporated
    milk

1 teaspoon allspice
¼ teaspoon ground cloves
pinch salt
½ cup raisins, chopped
1 unbaked 9-inch pie shell

Mix the pumpkin, eggs, sugar, evaporated milk, and spices together, blending well. Put into the pie shell and scatter the raisins evenly over the top. Bake on the middle rack of a 350° oven for 45 minutes.

Serves 8.

Thin Man Pie

During World War II, sugar was rationed or unavailable, but we always got Karo syrup for the babies. Since we had to have something sweet on the table, this is what we invented. The recipe makes two pies.

1 box (1 pound) brown sugar
1 cup Karo syrup
1 stick butter or margarine, melted

4 eggs, beaten
2 teaspoons vanilla extract
2 unbaked 9-inch pie shells

In a bowl, mix the sugar, Karo syrup, and butter, combining well. Stir in the eggs and vanilla. Mix well. Pour into the pie shells. Bake at 325° for 40 minutes or until set.

Each pie serves 8.

Mud Pie

This recipe makes two pies, but I don't think you'll have any problem getting rid of them at a family gathering.

1 box (18¼ ounces) German chocolate cake mix
1 stick margarine or butter, cut into pieces
1 package (8 ounces) cream cheese, cut into pieces
1 cup brown sugar, packed
2 cups chopped walnuts
1 can (3½ ounces) flake coconut

Grease two 9-inch pie pans. Prepare the cake batter according to package directions and spread evenly in the pans. In a saucepan over low heat, soften the cream cheese and margarine and combine well. Remove from heat and add the brown sugar, mixing well. Add the walnuts and coconut, stirring to mix. Using a spoon, place the cream cheese mixture evenly over the cake batter. Bake at 350° for 30 to 35 minutes.

Each pie serves 8.

Sweet Potato Pie

1½ pounds sweet potatoes
1½ sticks butter or margarine, softened
2 cups sugar
3 eggs beaten
½ teaspoon ginger

½ teaspoon nutmeg
½ teaspoon ground cloves
pinch salt
1 teaspoon vanilla extract
½ cup milk
1 unbaked 9-inch pie shell

Wash the sweet potatoes and place them in a pot, covered with water. Bring to a boil. When the potatoes are soft (after about 45 minutes), drain, cool, and peel. Using a fork or potato masher, mash the potatoes in a large bowl along with the margarine and sugar, combining well. Add the eggs. Stir in the spices, vanilla, and milk. Pour into the pie shell. Bake in a 375° oven for 45 minutes or until the center is firm.

Serves 8.

Old-Fashioned Potato Pie

1 can (1 pound, 13 ounces) whole
    sweet potatoes
1½ cups brown sugar, packed
1 stick butter, softened
½ cup dark Karo syrup
3 eggs, beaten
½ teaspoon ginger

1 teaspoon nutmeg
pinch salt
1 teaspoon vanilla extract
1 small can (5 ounces) evaporated
    milk
1 unbaked 10-inch pie shell

Drain the potatoes and mash them, working the brown sugar and butter into the potatoes as you mash. Stir in the Karo syrup and eggs, followed by the spices, vanilla, and evaporated milk, combining thoroughly. Pour into the pie shell and bake in a 375° oven for 45 minutes or until the center is firm.

Serves 10 to 12.

Note: You can also prepare this as two small pies, using 5-inch frozen crusts.

Cobbler Crust

Follow the general procedures here for making the crust and baking the cobbler in all the cobbler recipes that follow. The procedures here call for a crust on top and bottom, but if you prefer, you can omit the bottom crust, placing the fruit mixture directly in the bottom of the dish and having a top crust only.

3 cups plain flour
½ teaspoon salt
2 tablespoons sugar

1 cup shortening
¼ cup cold water

Put the flour, salt, and sugar in a bowl. Add the shortening and mix everything together well, using a fork or your fingertips, until crumbly. Add the water and mix to form a moist ball of dough. On a floured board, roll out half of the dough to make a crust that fits the bottom of the dish in which the cobbler is being made. Press the crust into the baking dish, prick it with a fork a few times, and bake in a 375° oven for 10 minutes. It should look done but not brown. Cool 10 to 12 minutes, then put the fruit mixture on top. Roll out the rest of the dough, place it on top of the fruit, and prick it with a fork a few times. Or roll it out, cut it into strips, and make a lattice crust over the fruit. If you like, brush the top crust with melted butter and sprinkle with sugar. Bake the cobbler at 375° for about 40 to 45 minutes (or as specified in the recipe), until the crust is well browned.

Granny Smith Apple Cobbler

3 pounds Granny Smith apples
1¼ cups sugar
pinch salt
1 teaspoon nutmeg

1 tablespoon flour
¾ stick butter or margarine
½ cup water
cobbler crust (see recipe above)

Preheat oven to 375°. Peel, core, and slice the apples and place them in a 10 × 10-inch baking dish, over a bottom crust if you like. Mix the sugar, salt, nutmeg, and flour together and spread over the apples. Pour the water over the apples and dot with the butter. Put a crust over the apple mixture and bake for 40 to 45 minutes.

Serves 8 to 10.

Pear Cobbler

Backyard pears are best for this cobbler, but, wherever you get your pears, always use ones that are ripe. Cobblers, in general, are especially good when cooked and reheated.

5 cups peeled, cored, and thinly
    sliced pears
1 tablespoon self-rising flour
1 cup sugar

⅛ teaspoon ginger
½ stick butter
¾ cup water
cobbler crust (see recipe above)

Preheat oven to 375°. Spread the sliced pears over the bottom of a 10 × 10-inch baking pan (or over a crust at the bottom of the dish). Mix the flour, sugar, and ginger together and sprinkle over the pears. Pour the water evenly over the pears. Dot with the butter. Place the top crust over the pear mixture and bake on the lower rack of the oven for 40 to 45 minutes.

Serves 8 to 10.

Blackberry Cobbler

Blackberries still grow wild in many places, so go out and pick your own.

5 cups blackberries	pinch salt
¾ cup sugar	½ stick butter or margarine
1 tablespoon flour	cobbler crust (see recipe above)
pinch ginger	

Preheat oven to 375°. Wash the blackberries, drain them, and put them into a baking dish or 10 × 10-inch pan (over a crust if you like). Mix the sugar, flour, ginger, and salt together. Pour over the berries and stir to mix well. Dot the berries with the butter. Place a crust over the berries and bake for 35 to 40 minutes.

Serves 8 to 10.

Fresh Strawberry-Rhubarb Cobbler

3 stalks rhubarb (about 3 cups cut-up)	¼ teaspoon salt
1 quart fresh strawberries	2 tablespoons cornstarch
2½ cups sugar	½ stick butter or margarine
	cobbler crust (see recipe above)

Preheat oven to 375°. Peel the rhubarb and cut it into ½-inch slices. Hull and wash the strawberries; cut them up if they are very large. Place on a paper towel to drain. Combine the strawberries and rhubarb slices in a bowl. Mix the sugar, salt, and cornstarch together and stir them into the berries and rhubarb. Put into a 9 × 13-inch baking dish (over a bottom crust if you wish) and dot with the butter. Place a top crust over the fruit and bake on the lower rack of the oven for 40 to 50 minutes.

Serves 10 to 12.

Fresh Strawberry Cobbler

1 quart fresh strawberries
1 small package (3 ounces)
   strawberry Jell-O
¾ cup sugar

pinch salt
1 tablespoon cornstarch
½ stick butter or margarine
cobbler crust (see recipe above)

Preheat oven to 375°. Hull and wash the strawberries. Cut them up if they are very large. Place on a paper towel to drain. Mix the Jell-O, sugar, salt, and cornstarch together and stir into the berries. Put the berries into a 1½-quart baking dish, with or without a bottom crust, as you prefer. Dot the berries with the butter. Put a crust over the strawberry mixture and bake on the lower rack of the oven for 40 to 45 minutes.

Serves 8 to 10.

Sweet Potato Cobbler

A real down-home dessert.

4 medium sweet potatoes,
   peeled and sliced thin
½ teaspoon ginger
1 cup brown sugar, packed
½ cup granulated sugar

1 heaping tablespoon flour
1 cup water
¾ stick butter or margarine
cobbler crust (see recipe above)

Preheat oven to 375°. Put the sweet potato slices in a 9 × 12-inch baking dish, spreading them over a bottom crust if you like. Mix together the ginger, both kinds of sugar, and the flour and sprinkle them over the potatoes. Dot the potatoes with the butter and add the water. Place a crust over the potatoes and bake for about 40 to 50 minutes.

Serves 10 to 12.

Fresh Peach Cobbler

When making peach cobbler, be sure to taste the peaches. The riper the peaches, the sweeter they will be, which means you should use less sugar. If the peaches are tangy, add a pinch of salt.

2 tablespoons self-rising flour
¼ teaspoon ginger
1 cup sugar

6 cups sliced fresh ripe peaches
¾ stick butter or margarine
cobbler crust (see recipe above)

Preheat oven to 375°. Mix the flour, ginger, and sugar together, pour over the peaches in a bowl, and mix well. Put the peach mixture in a 9 × 12-inch baking dish, over a bottom crust. Dot the peaches with the butter. Place a top crust over the peaches and bake on the lower rack of the oven for 35 to 40 minutes.

Serves 8.

Peach Betty

2 cans sliced peaches, drained
1 cup graham cracker crumbs
¼ stick margarine or butter

Place the peaches in an 8 × 8-inch baking dish. Melt the butter and mix it evenly into the graham cracker crumbs. Spread the buttered crumbs over the peaches. Bake at 350° for 30 minutes.

Serves 6.

Apple Betty

Use Washington State or Rome apples.

6 cups peeled, sliced apples
¾ cup sugar
1 teaspoon lemon extract
1 cup grated cheddar cheese

½ stick butter or margarine,
    melted
1¼ cups graham cracker crumbs

Preheat oven to 400°. Mix together the apples, sugar, and lemon extract and place in a 9 × 13-inch baking pan. Combine the cheese, butter, and graham cracker crumbs, stirring to mix evenly, and spread over the apples. Bake on the lowest rack of the oven for 35 minutes.

Serves 8 to 10.

Coconut Tarts

These tarts sell well at school fund-raising events.

1 cup sugar
2 teaspoons flour
1 teaspoon nutmeg
1 large can (12 ounces) evaporated
    milk

3 eggs beaten
1 teaspoon vanilla extract
pinch salt
1 package (7 ounces) flake coconut
tart shells

Combine the sugar, flour, and nutmeg. Add the evaporated milk, eggs, vanilla, salt, and coconut. Mix well. Pour into tart shells, stirring to distribute the coconut evenly. Bake at 375° for 30 to 35 minutes.

Makes about 15.

Aunt Mary's Old-Fashioned Stacked Double-Crust Applesauce Pie

This was made with homegrown apples that ripened about the middle of August or early September. Buy tart apples such as Rome or Fuji to make this pie. Aunt Mary made her stacks three high, but some people stacked theirs six high.

6 cups peeled, sliced apples
½ cup water
1¼ cups sugar
¾ stick butter or margarine,
   cut into pieces

2 tablespoons flour
1 teaspoon nutmeg
½ teaspoon lemon extract
2 recipes double pie crust dough

Preheat oven to 375°. Cook the apples in the water, stirring to cook evenly, until just tender. Remove from heat and add the sugar, butter, flour, nutmeg, and lemon extract. Mix well. Roll out the dough; reserve half for the top crust and use half to form a crust in the bottom of two 9-inch pie pans; prick the crusts a few times with a fork and bake for 10 to 12 minutes. Let cool. Put the apple mixture on top of the baked crusts, dividing it evenly between the two pies. Place the top crust over the apples, seal the edges, and prick the crust a few times with a fork. Bake until the crust is brown, about 45 minutes. When cool, remove the pies from the pans and stack one on top of the other to make a double-stacked single pie.

Serves 12.

Blueberry Dream

The sour cream topping makes this a truly special dessert.

5 cups fresh blueberries
½ cup sugar
1 tablespoon fresh lemon juice
¼ teaspoon grated lemon rind
1 cup graham cracker crumbs
½ stick butter or margarine,
    melted

TOPPING:
1 cup sour cream
¼ cup 10x powdered sugar
1 teaspoon lemon juice (optional)

Make the topping by stirring the sugar into the sour cream until well combined. Stir in the lemon juice if you'd like the topping a little tart. Refrigerate until ready to use.

Preheat oven to 400°. Wash and drain the blueberries. In a 1½-quart baking dish or pan, mix together the blueberries, sugar, lemon juice, and lemon rind. Spread them evenly in the dish. Mix together the graham cracker crumbs and butter and spread evenly over the blueberries. Bake on the lower rack of the oven for 35 to 40 minutes, until the buttered crumbs are lightly brown. Serve warm, with the topping.

Serves 8.

Puddings

Banana Pudding

2 pounds bananas, ripe but not mushy
vanilla wafers (about 3 dozen)
2 cups milk (skim milk if you like)
1 can (14 ounces) sweetened condensed milk
1 family-size box (4.6 ounces) cook and serve vanilla pudding mix
1 teaspoon vanilla extract

Slice the bananas and layer them with the vanilla wafers in a 1½-quart casserole dish. Mix the milk and sweetened condensed milk together in a saucepan and let them get hot over medium heat but do not let them come to a boil. Using a wire whisk, stir in the pudding mix. Cook only until the pudding begins to thicken. Remove from the heat, add the vanilla, and pour over the bananas and vanilla wafers. Crush a few vanilla wafers and sprinkle them over the top. Serve warm.

Serves 8.

World War II Banana Pudding

This banana pudding was made with Karo syrup and Pet milk when sugar was rationed during World War II. My favorite. Use bread ends or sliced biscuits for the bread cubes.

2 pounds bananas
3 tablespoons flour
½ cup sugar
1 large can (12 ounces) Pet
    evaporated milk
1 can water
1 cup dark Karo syrup

3 egg yolks
2 teaspoons vanilla extract
4 cups bread cubes

MERINGUE:
3 egg whites
2 tablespoons sugar

Mix the flour and sugar together in a bowl. Combine the Pet milk, water, and Karo syrup in a saucepan and heat over medium heat just to the boiling point. Using a wire whisk, stir the flour and sugar mixture into the saucepan. Remove from the heat and slowly add the egg yolks, stirring with the whisk as you add them. Return the pan to the heat and cook for 3 minutes, stirring constantly, or until well heated and creamy. Cut the bananas into ½-inch slices. Layer them with the bread cubes in the bottom of a 1½-quart baking dish, ending with bread cubes on top. Pour the custard mix over the bananas and bread.

To make the meringue, beat the egg whites with an electric mixer on high speed; slowly add the sugar, beating until the whites are stiff. Spread over the top of the custard. Brown in a 400° oven for about 10 minutes.

Serves 8.

Sweet Potato Pudding

You can't beat this old-time favorite. When sugar was rationed during World War II, we used Karo syrup in its place.

4 cups grated raw, peeled sweet
   potatoes
1 stick butter or margarine, melted
½ teaspoon ground cloves
½ teaspoon ginger
½ teaspoon allspice
3 eggs, beaten

1 cup brown sugar, packed
1 cup dark Karo syrup
1¼ cups milk
½ cup pecan pieces, raisins, or
   coconut, or any of the three in
   combination (optional)

Preheat oven to 350°. Combine the sweet potatoes, butter, spices, eggs, brown sugar, Karo syrup, and milk. Stir to mix well. Add the nuts, raisins, or coconut, if you like. Pour into a greased 1-quart baking dish and bake for 50 to 60 minutes or until well set.

Serves 8 to 10.

Pineapple Snow Pudding

An old-fashioned but easy dessert.

1 angel food cake
3 cups milk
1 large box (4.6 ounces) cook and
   serve vanilla pudding mix
3 egg yolks
¼ cup sugar

2 teaspoons vanilla extract
1 large can (20 ounces) crushed
   pineapple, drained
1 package (6 ounces) frozen grated
   coconut

Slice the cake and cut it into squares or just pinch it into irregular pieces and place in a baking dish. In a saucepan, heat the milk until hot but not

boiling. Stir in the pudding mix and add egg yolks slowly, stirring constantly. Let cook, stirring, until thickened. Remove from the heat and
stir in the sugar and vanilla. Stir in the pineapple and pour over the cake
in the baking dish. Sprinkle the coconut on top. Refrigerate until ready
to serve.

Serves 8 to 10.

Chocolate Pudding

*Serve this pudding hot with vanilla ice cream. Good for teen get-togethers
or a dessert party with good coffee. We always had cocoa in our house!*

½ cup cocoa	2 sticks butter, melted
1½ cups sugar	4 cups boiling water
2 cups self-rising flour	½ cup walnuts (optional)

Preheat oven to 400°. In a large bowl, mix together the cocoa and sugar.
Add the flour and mash out any lumps. Add the butter and boiling
water (and the walnuts if desired) and mix well. Pour into a 10 × 10-inch
baking pan. Sprinkle over with sugar to make a little crispy topping.
Bake for 30 minutes.

Serves 8 to 10.

Rum Raisin Bread Pudding

Old fashioned but with a new taste.

1 cup sugar
½ stick butter or margarine,
   melted
4 eggs, beaten
2 cups milk
1 teaspoon nutmeg

3 tablespoons rum
   (or a minibottle)
4 cups bread cubes
1 cup raisins
plain yogurt

Preheat oven to 375°. Mix together the sugar and butter and add the eggs. Mix well. Add the milk, nutmeg, and rum, stirring until well combined. Stir in the bread cubes and raisins. Let sit for 5 to 10 minutes and stir again. Pour into a 2-quart baking dish or pan. Bake for 35 to 40 minutes. Serve topped with plain yogurt.

Serves 8 to 10.

Pineapple Bread Pudding

1 cup sugar
¾ stick margarine, melted
3 eggs beaten
1 large can (12 ounces) evaporated
   milk

1 large can (20 ounces) crushed
   pineapple
5 cups bread crumbs

Preheat oven to 375°. Mix the sugar and margarine together in a large bowl. Add the eggs, evaporated milk, and pineapple. Mix well. Stir in the bread crumbs. Pour into a 2-quart baking dish and bake for 30 to 40 minutes.

Serves 8.

Wild Persimmon Pudding

Persimmons are found in the woods among other trees. They bear orange frosty fruit that get ripe in October and have 4 flat seeds. It will take about a half gallon of ripe persimmons to make 3–4 cups of pulp.

3–4 cups persimmon pulp
  (use very ripe persimmons)
2 eggs
2 cups brown sugar, packed
1 cup milk
2 cups self-rising flour

1 stick butter
1 teaspoon vanilla extract
1 teaspoon cinnamon
½ cup raisins, chopped (optional)
1 cup chopped walnuts (optional)

Preheat oven to 350°. Wash the persimmons under cold running water. Remove the seeds and set aside for 20 minutes. Mash the persimmons through a colander or strainer to make a pulp. (If the persimmons are very nice, you can just remove the seeds and put the persimmons in a blender to process.) Beat the eggs, adding the sugar, until well mixed. Add the milk, alternating with the flour, in thirds, combining well. Add the vanilla and cinnamon. Stir in the persimmons (and raisins and walnuts, if used). Mix well. Melt the butter in a 1½-quart baking dish or 9 × 12-inch pan and tilt the pan to coat the bottom and sides with butter. Pour the persimmon mixture into the pan. Bake for 1 hour or until firm. Serve with whipped topping.

Serves 6.

Stewed Yard Peaches, Cherries, or Apples

6 cups peeled, sliced apples or ripe peaches, or 4 cups cherries, pitted
¾ cup sugar
½ cup water

Mix the fruit, sugar, and water together in a pot. Bring to a boil, then turn the heat to low and let the fruit simmer for 10 minutes. Serve warm.

Serves 4 to 6.

Cookies

Molasses Cookies

In the winter, when the snow was on the ground, Roland would make molasses cookie dough and spread it out over large biscuit pans with his hands and bake it in the oven. When the cow was milked, the milk would be strained into a stone jar and set outside to get cold. Before bedtime, by the fireplace, we played a game called "heavy, heavy, hang over your head," where you had to quack like a duck, or cluck, or meow, or do something like that to get your treat of warm molasses cookies and milk.

1 cup sugar
1 cup shortening
1 cup molasses
½ cup milk
3–4 cups self-rising flour

1 teaspoon baking soda
½ teaspoon salt
1 teaspoon ginger
1 teaspoon allspice
2 eggs, beaten

Mix the sugar, shortening, molasses, and milk together in a saucepan. Bring to a boil and simmer 2 minutes. Cool. Sift together the flour, baking soda, salt, ginger, and allspice. Add the eggs to the cooled molasses mixture. Add the dry ingredients. Mix well—I use my fingers—to make a dough firm enough to roll. On a floured board, roll out the dough to ¼ inch thickness. Cut out individual cookies with a 3-inch cookie or biscuit cutter and place them on a lightly greased cookie sheet, 1 inch apart. Bake at 375° for 8 to 10 minutes, just until the cookies are firm.

Makes about 5 dozen.

Krispie Crunches

1 cup margarine, softened
1 cup brown sugar, packed
1 cup granulated sugar
2 eggs, beaten
2 cups sifted self-rising flour
1 teaspoon salt

½ teaspoon baking soda
1 teaspoon vanilla extract
2 cups quick oatmeal
2 cups Rice Krispies
1 cup flake coconut
1 cup chocolate chips

Preheat oven to 350°. Cream the shortening and both kinds of sugar, beating until light and fluffy. Add the eggs and beat well. Sift together the flour, salt, and baking soda; add them to the wet ingredients. Add the oatmeal, Rice Krispies, coconut, and chocolate chips. Mix well. The batter should be stiff. Roll the dough into small balls, place on a greased cookie sheet, and flatten with a fork, leaving about an inch between the flattened cookies. (Dip the fork into cold water as it becomes sticky.) Bake for 12 minutes.

Makes about 5 dozen.

Chocolate Chip Cookies

1 stick butter, softened
½ cup dark brown sugar, packed
½ cup granulated sugar
1 egg
1 teaspoon vanilla extract
1½ cups all-purpose flour

2 tablespoons cocoa
½ teaspoon baking soda
½ teaspoon salt
1 cup semisweet chocolate chips
½ cup chopped pecans

Preheat oven to 375°. In a bowl, beat together the butter and both kinds of sugar until light and fluffy. Add the egg and vanilla and mix well. Sift the flour, cocoa, baking soda, and salt together in a bowl. Add to the wet ingredients and mix well. Stir in the chocolate chips and pecans. Using a spoon, drop batter onto a greased cookie sheet, forming cookies of whatever size you prefer, leaving the cookies about 2 inches apart. Bake for 8 to 10 minutes, just until firm.

Makes 4 dozen 2-inch cookies.

One-Room School Tea Cookies

Tea cookies and cocoa were served for our Christmas parties at school. My sister Bernice made these cookies.

1 cup butter, softened
2 cups sugar
4 eggs, beaten
5 cups self-rising flour

½ teaspoon baking powder
2 teaspoons lemon extract
2 tablespoons milk

Preheat oven to 350°. Cream the butter and sugar together until light and fluffy with a wooden spoon or a mixer. Beat in the eggs. Sift the flour and baking powder together, then combine with the creamed mixture, lemon extract, and milk. Mix well with your fingers. Roll the dough out ¼ inch thick and cut into individual cookies with a 2-inch biscuit cutter. Bake on an ungreased cookie sheet for about 10 minutes, just until firm. Sprinkle with a little sugar. Remove from the cookie sheet and cool on brown paper.

Makes about 3 dozen.

Butterscotch Brownies

1 stick butter
2 cups brown sugar, packed
2 eggs, beaten
1 teaspoon vanilla extract

1 cup all-purpose flour
½ teaspoon salt
2 teaspoons baking powder
1 cup chopped walnuts

Preheat oven to 375°. Lightly butter a 9 × 9-inch baking pan. In a saucepan, melt the butter over low heat. Add the sugar and stir to mix. Remove from the heat and let cool a bit. When the mixture is no longer hot but still warm, stir in the eggs and vanilla. Sift together the flour, salt, and baking powder and add to the wet ingredients. Fold in the walnuts. Pour into the baking pan and bake for 25 minutes until browned. Let cool and cut into squares.

Makes 12 to 16.

Chocolate Brownies

1 stick butter, softened
1 cup sugar
2 eggs
2 squares unsweetened chocolate
½ cup all-purpose flour

½ teaspoon salt
½ teaspoon baking powder
1 teaspoon vanilla extract
1 cup chopped black walnuts

Preheat oven to 375°. Melt the chocolate in a microwave or double boiler. Let cool. Cream the butter and sugar together with a wooden spoon or a mixer until light and fluffy. Beat in the eggs until well mixed. Stir in the chocolate. Sift together the flour, salt, and baking powder and add them to the wet ingredients. Mix well. Add the vanilla and stir 8 to 10 strokes. Stir in the nuts. Pour into an 8 × 8-inch baking pan and bake for 25 minutes or until done. Let cool and cut into squares.

Makes 12 to 16.

Beverages

On the farm, fresh milk and buttermilk, plus well or spring water, were always on the table at mealtime for each person to pick from, as desired. My customers often ask me just how I make my refreshing lemonade or iced tea. I always say, "There's nothing special," and I'm happy to tell anyone how I make it—so I've included the recipes here. Mama Dip's Kitchen now serves a selection of beers and wines, but I remember back when country folks all made their own. Who didn't make some kind of spirit drink in Chatham County? People made locust beer, home brew, corn wine, tomato wine, muscadine wine, or blackberry wine. To make wine, the grapes or berries harvested in summer or early fall would be put in a wash pot with a little water and cooked real slow for hours, mixed with sugar, then covered in the pot and left to sit overnight. The next day, the mixture was poured into crock jars, which then sat covered until Thanksgiving. Finally, the wine would be strained and stored in quart jars. Some would be kept for years!

Brunch Champagne Punch

This is what my daughters serve at parties at home. When we offered brunch at the restaurant, we served this.

2 bottles champagne, chilled
1 can (46 ounces) mango and orange juice, chilled

Combine the champagne and juice in a punch bowl. Add orange slices to float in the bowl.

Serves 20.

Mama Dip's Patio Cooler

When the restaurant had a bar, this was the best-selling drink at Dip's.

4 ounces Southern Comfort
4 ounces Creme de Almond
2 ounces Triple Sec
2 ounces brandy
4 ounces pineapple juice
4 ounces orange juice
4 ounces sweet and sour mixer

Combine all the ingredients and pour over ice; garnish each glass with a lemon slice and a maraschino cherry, with stem.

Serves 6.

Bloody Mary Brunch Mix

Add a bit of horseradish for extra flavor.

2 quarts tomato juice
½ cup Worcestershire sauce

4 tablespoons celery salt
4 dashes Tabasco sauce

Combine all of the ingredients and reserve; mix with vodka and serve over ice.

Serves about 10.

Spiced Cider

This can be served hot or cold. Feel free to vary the amount of cider a little to suit your individual taste.

1 cup sugar
½ teaspoon ground cinnamon
½ teaspoon ground cloves
4 cups water
juice of 2 lemons
1 small can (6 ounces) frozen orange juice concentrate, undiluted
½ gallon cider (more can be used, if desired, especially to serve hot)

In a large pot, add the sugar and spices to the water and bring to a boil. Add the orange juice and cider. Remove the pot from the heat and cover. Let the cider sit for 5 to 10 minutes before serving warm, or let the cider cool and then refrigerate until ready to serve.

Serves 10 to 15.

Party Time Fruit Punch

4 packages cherry-flavored Kool-Aid mix (unsweetened)
2 cans (46 ounces each) pineapple juice, chilled
1 large can (12 ounces) frozen orange juice concentrate, undiluted
2½ cups sugar
4 quarts water
4 quarts ginger ale, chilled

Mix all of the ingredients together in a large punch bowl. When ready to serve, add a block of ice to the bowl.

Serves 20 teenagers.

Grape-Lemon Kool-Aid

A family tradition—this is what my children were raised on.

Make up a pitcher of powdered grape drink (such as sweetened grape Kool-Aid) according to package directions. Add the juice of 1 lemon and the lemon peel, sliced fine. Serve on ice.

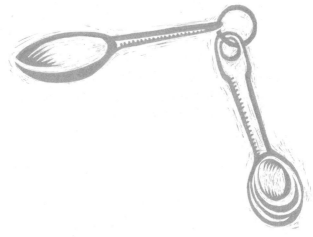

Fresh-Squeezed Lemonade

Buy lemons that are bright yellow and let them ripen out of the refrigerator for two days.

6 lemons
1½ cups sugar
2 quarts water

Squeeze the juice from the lemons; reserve the peels. Remove the seeds and pour the juice into a 2-quart pitcher. Add the sugar and 1 quart of the water. Stir to dissolve the sugar. Slice the peels from all 6 lemons and put them into the pitcher. Stir in the other quart of water. Serve on ice.

Serves about 6.

Iced Tea

You can vary this recipe in a couple of ways, if you like. You can use light brown sugar as a sweetener for a milder sweet tea. For lemon tea, add a package of lemonade drink mix.

6 family-size tea bags
1 quart boiling water

1 cup sugar
1 quart cold water

Drop the tea bags into the boiling water in a pot. Turn off the heat and let sit for 15 to 20 minutes. Pour the tea into a pitcher, add the sugar, and stir. Rinse the tea bags with a little warm water and squeeze them against the side of the pot with the back of a spoon. Add cold water to make 1 quart. Pour into the pitcher.

Serves about 6.

Party Dishes

Pound Cake Sundae

1 pound cake (fresh or frozen)
1 jar (16 ounces) hot fudge sauce
vanilla ice cream

1 can (7 ounces) whipped topping
chopped walnuts (optional)

Heat the fudge. Cut the pound cake into 1-inch slices. Toast the slices
in the toaster or oven. For each serving, scoop ice cream onto a slice of
pound cake while the cake is still warm. Spoon hot fudge over the ice
cream and top with whipped topping. Sprinkle on walnuts if you wish.

Strawberry Cake

1 box (18¼ ounces) white cake mix
1 small box (3 ounces) strawberry
  Jell-O
3 tablespoons flour
4 eggs
¾ cup vegetable oil
½ cup water
¾ cup mashed ripe strawberries

ICING:
1 stick butter, softened
½ cup mashed ripe strawberries
1 box (1 pound) 10x powdered
  sugar

Mix the cake mix, flour, and Jell-O together in a bowl. Add the other
ingredients, beating with an electric mixer as directed on the cake mix
package about 5 minutes. Bake in a greased 9 × 9-inch pan at 350° for
20 to 25 minutes. Cool before icing.

   To make the icing, combine all of the ingredients. Add a little milk if
needed to achieve a proper spreading consistency.

Serves 12.

Party Shrimp

1 stick butter or margarine
2 teaspoons garlic salt
1½ pounds raw shrimp, peeled
  and deveined

2 tablespoons Worcestershire
  sauce
2 tablespoons chopped fresh
  parsley

Melt the butter in a pan, but do not let it brown. Mix in the garlic salt.
Add the shrimp and cook, stirring, over medium heat, for about 8 minutes, until the shrimp begin to turn pink. Do not overcook. Add the
Worcestershire sauce. Stir to mix. Turn off the heat, cover, and let sit for
4 to 5 minutes. Sprinkle on the parsley. Pierce each shrimp with a toothpick or place the shrimp in a serving dish with toothpicks alongside so
guests can help themselves. Serve warm or cold.

Serves 8.

Cheese Ball with Ham

½ pound sharp cheddar cheese,
  grated
8 ounces cream cheese, softened
¼ cup blue cheese salad dressing
1 tablespoon Worcestershire sauce

4 ounces ham luncheon meat
  slices, finely chopped
¼ teaspoon garlic salt
chopped fresh parsley

Mix all of the ingredients except the parsley together well. Shape into a
ball and roll in the chopped parsley. Refrigerate until ready to serve with
crackers.

Serves 15 to 20.

Stuffed Banana Peppers

8 banana peppers
1 package (8 ounces) cream
   cheese, softened
1 tablespoon grated carrots
1 cucumber, seeded and finely
   chopped
1 tablespoon finely chopped
   spring onion
1 tablespoon chopped parsley
1 teaspoon chopped chives

Mix all the ingredients except the peppers together in a bowl. Set aside. Cut the peppers in half lengthwise and remove the seeds. The peppers should be dry when they're stuffed, so wipe off any moisture with a paper towel. Stuff the peppers with the cream cheese mixture and slice into bite-size pieces (about 1 inch square).

Serves about 16.

Deviled Eggs

6 eggs, hard boiled
1 teaspoon prepared mustard
2 tablespoons mayonnaise
2 tablespoons sweet pickle relish
¼ teaspoon salt
dash black pepper

With a sharp knife, cut the eggs in half and lay them on a platter. Carefully remove the egg yolks, leaving the whites intact, and add them to all the other ingredients in a bowl, mixing well. Spoon the mixture evenly into the egg whites.

Makes 12.

Council Childhood Birthday Party

Having a birthday party for children does not have to be expensive. For $15.00, you can give your child a good-time party. Remembering that it is his or her birthday, let your child choose which friends to invite—usually no more than 10. A small party is easy to manage.

1 cake made from a mix as
   directed and baked in a
   9 × 13-inch baking pan
1 can frosting
1 quart ice cream
2 packs of Kool-Aid punch,
   made as directed
ice from the freezer
paper plates, cups, and napkins
plastic forks and spoons

a package of balloons
a present for the birthday boy
   or girl
games to play
plenty of time to play and talk
a thank-you gift, in a sandwich
   bag, of lollipops, candy corn,
   lifesavers, and bubble gum for
   each guest to take home

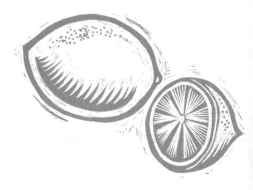

Index